Hamas: Background and Issues for Congress

Jim Zanotti
Analyst in Middle Eastern Affairs

December 2, 2010

Congressional Research Service

7-5700

www.crs.gov

R41514

CRS Report for Congress ———————————————————————

Prepared for Members and Committees of Congress

Summary

This report and its appendixes provide background information on Hamas, or the Islamic Resistance Movement, and U.S. policy towards it. It also includes information and analysis on (1) the threats Hamas currently poses to U.S. interests, (2) how Hamas compares with other Middle East terrorist groups, (3) Hamas's ideology and policies (both generally and on discrete issues), (4) its leadership and organization, and (5) its sources of assistance. Finally, the report raises and discusses various legislative and oversight options related to foreign aid strategies, financial sanctions, and regional and international political approaches. In evaluating these options, Congress can assess how Hamas has emerged and adapted over time, and also scrutinize the track record of U.S., Israeli, and international policy to counter Hamas.

Hamas is a Palestinian Islamist military and sociopolitical movement that grew out of the Muslim Brotherhood. The United States, Israel, the European Union, and Canada consider Hamas a terrorist organization because of (1) its violent resistance to what it deems Israeli occupation of historic Palestine (constituting present-day Israel, West Bank, and Gaza Strip), and (2) its rejection of the off-and-on peace process involving Israel and the Palestine Liberation Organization (PLO) since the early 1990s. Since Hamas's inception in 1987, it has maintained its primary base of political support and its military command in the Gaza Strip—a territory it has controlled since June 2007—while also having a significant presence in the West Bank. The movement's political leadership is currently headquartered in exile in Damascus, Syria. Hamas receives assistance and training from Iran, Syria, and the Lebanese Shiite militant group Hezbollah. Hamas is often discussed alongside other groups in the region that engage in militant and terrorist activities to achieve their ends, yet Hamas has confined its militancy to Israel and the Palestinian territories—distinguishing it from the broader aspirations expressed by Al Qaeda and its affiliates.

The overarching U.S. goal regarding Hamas is to deter, transform, marginalize, or neutralize it so that it no longer presents a threat to Israel's security, to a peaceful and lasting resolution of the Israeli-Palestinian conflict, or to other U.S. interests—either in its own right or as a proxy of Iran or other actors. Various legislative and policy initiatives designed to accomplish this goal have at most achieved temporary or partial success. It is possible to conclude that U.S. and other international support for Israel and the Palestinian Authority/PLO dominated by Fatah (Hamas's main rival faction) has been counterproductive to some extent when comparing Hamas's domestic, regional, and international strength in the early 1990s—measured by factors such as popularity, military force, and leverage with other actors (including Israel and Fatah)—to its current strength. The Israeli-Egyptian closure regime in Gaza and various U.S. and international initiatives constrain and isolate Hamas to a point and may exacerbate its internal organizational tensions and tactical disagreements. Yet, the threats Hamas continues to pose to Israel, to prospects for a two-state solution and to the future of Palestinian democracy present considerable risks and difficult trade-offs for any U.S. policy decisions going forward.

The following CRS reports contain additional information on Hamas: CRS Report RL34074, *The Palestinians: Background and U.S. Relations*, by Jim Zanotti; CRS Report R40101, *Israel and Hamas: Conflict in Gaza (2008-2009)*, coordinated by Jim Zanotti; CRS Report R40092, *Israel and the Palestinians: Prospects for a Two-State Solution*, by Jim Zanotti; CRS Report R40664, *U.S. Security Assistance to the Palestinian Authority*, by Jim Zanotti; and CRS Report RS22967, *U.S. Foreign Aid to the Palestinians*, by Jim Zanotti.

Contents

Figures

Tables

Appendixes

Contacts

Introduction: Issues for Congress

Hamas,[1] or the Islamic Resistance Movement, is a Palestinian Islamist military and sociopolitical movement that grew out of the Muslim Brotherhood, a Sunni religious and political organization founded in Egypt in 1928 that has branches throughout the world. The United States, Israel, the European Union, and Canada consider Hamas a terrorist organization because of (1) its violent resistance to what it deems Israeli occupation of historic Palestine (constituting present-day Israel, West Bank, and Gaza Strip), and (2) its rejection of the off-and-on peace process involving Israel and the Palestine Liberation Organization (PLO) since the early 1990s. Hamas seeks assistance and training from other Arab, Islamic, and international actors and organizations, and receives it from Iran, Syria, and the Lebanese Shiite militant group Hezbollah (see "Iran, Syria, and Hezbollah" below).[2]

The overarching U.S. goal regarding Hamas is to deter, transform, marginalize, or neutralize it so that it no longer presents a threat to Israel's security, to a peaceful and lasting resolution of the Israeli-Palestinian conflict, or to other U.S. interests—either in its own right or as a proxy of Iran or other actors. Various legislative and policy initiatives designed to accomplish this goal have at most achieved temporary or partial success. Hamas's activities present challenges for U.S. policymakers and members of Congress, including

- countering Hamas's military and terrorist threats to Israel, its financial and smuggling networks, and its political influence;

- determining under what circumstances and the manner in which the United States might accept the participation of Hamas or Hamas representatives in a Palestinian Authority (PA) government and/or in Israeli-Palestinian peace negotiations;

- de-linking Hamas from its connections with Iran and Syria; and

- encouraging humanitarian relief efforts and economic development in Gaza without bolstering Hamas.

U.S. efforts and policy debates on these issues, which include foreign aid strategies, financial sanctions, and bilateral, regional, and international political approaches, are discussed further below (see "Possible Options for Congress").

-

---

[1] Hamas is the transliterated acronym for the group's Arabic name, "Harakat al Muqawama al Islamiyya," or the "Islamic Resistance Movement." The acronym "Hamas" itself is an Arabic word meaning "zeal."

[2] See U.S. State Department, "Country Reports on Terrorism 2009," Chapter 6. Terrorist Organizations, available at http://www.state.gov/s/ct/rls/crt/2009/140900.htm: "HAMAS receives some funding, weapons, and training from Iran. In addition, fundraising takes place in the Persian Gulf countries, but the group also receives donations from Palestinian expatriates around the world. Some fundraising and propaganda activity takes place in Western Europe and North America. Syria provides safe haven for its leadership." See also Anna Fitfield, "Hizbollah Confirms Broad Aid for Hamas," *Financial Times*, May 12, 2009.

Figure 1. Map of Key Hamas Leadership Nodes

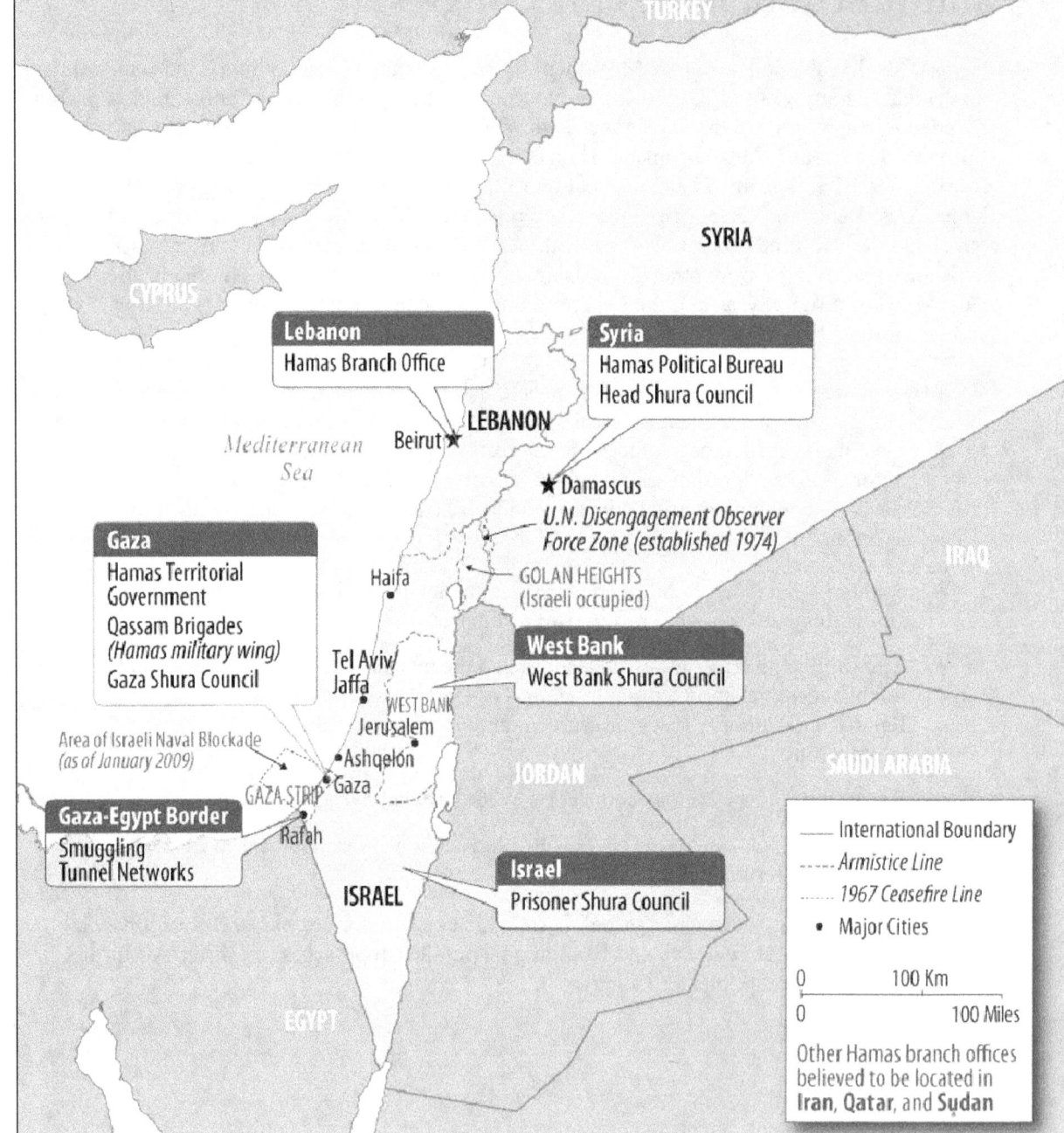

Sources: Congressional Research Service; State of Israel, Ministry of Transport, Notice to Mariners, No. 1/2009 Blockade of Gaza Strip, January 2009; ESRI Community Data, 2008.

Notes: All boundaries and depictions are approximate. The designations employed and the presentation of material on this map do not imply the expression of any opinion whatsoever on the part of CRS concerning the legal status of any country, territory, city or area or of its authorities, or concerning the delimitation of its frontiers of boundaries.

Overview

Since Hamas's inception in 1987, it has maintained its primary base of political support and its military command in the Gaza Strip—a territory it has controlled since June 2007—while also having a significant presence in the West Bank. The movement's political leadership is currently headquartered in exile in Damascus, Syria.

Hamas's military wing, the Izz al Din al Qassam Brigades,[3] has killed more than 400 Israelis,[4] and at least 25 U.S. citizens (including some dual U.S.-Israeli citizens)[5] in attacks since 1993. As the Qassam Brigades developed from a small band of guerrillas into a more sophisticated organization with access to greater resources and territorial control, its methods of attack evolved from small-scale kidnappings and killings of Israeli military personnel to suicide bombings and rocket attacks against Israeli civilians. Hamas also has frequently attacked or repressed Palestinian political and factional opponents, particularly in its struggle with Fatah and other groups for control in the Gaza Strip since Israel's military disengagement in 2005. For further information on these points, see "Threats Hamas Poses," **Appendix A**, and **Appendix B** below.

Hamas emerged as the main domestic opposition force to Palestinian nationalist leader Yasser Arafat and his secular nationalist Fatah movement in the West Bank and Gaza Strip in the 1980s and 1990s—largely by using violence against Israeli civilian and military targets just as Arafat's PLO began negotiating with Israel. In 2006, a little more than a year after Arafat's death and the election of Fatah's Mahmoud Abbas to replace him as PA president, Hamas became—by most analysts' reckoning—the first Islamist group in the Arab world to gain power democratically after a stunning electoral upset of Fatah gave it control of the Palestinian Legislative Council (PLC) and of Palestinian Authority government ministries.[6]

Subsequent efforts by Israel, the United States, and the international community to neutralize or marginalize Hamas by military, political, and economic means may have changed the outward nature of its influence, but have failed to squelch it. In 2007, Hamas seized control of the Gaza Strip through decisive armed victories over PA and Fatah forces loyal to Abbas (causing Abbas to dismiss Hamas's PA government in the West Bank and appoint a "caretaker" non-Hamas government in its stead). Hamas has since consolidated its power in Gaza despite considerable damage visited on Gaza's people and infrastructure by an Israeli invasion in December 2008-

---

[3] Izz Al Din al Qassam was a Muslim Brotherhood member, preacher, and leader of an anti-Zionist and anti-colonialist resistance movement in historic Palestine during the British Mandate period. He was killed by British forces on November 19, 1935.

[4] Figures culled from Israel Ministry of Foreign Affairs website at http://www.mfa.gov.il/MFA/Terrorism-+Obstacle+to+Peace/Palestinian+terror+before+2000/
Suicide%20and%20Other%20Bombing%20Attacks%20in%20Israel%20Since and
http://www.mfa.gov.il/MFA/Terrorism-+Obstacle+to+Peace/Palestinian+terror+since+2000/Victims+of+Palestinian+Violence+and+Terrorism+sinc.htm; and from Jewish Virtual Library website at http://www.jewishvirtuallibrary.org/jsource/Terrorism/TerrorAttacks.html. In the aggregate, other Palestinian militant groups (such as Palestinian Islamic Jihad, the Fatah-affiliated Al Aqsa Martyrs' Brigades, and the Popular Front for the Liberation of Palestine) also have killed scores, if not hundreds, of Israelis since 1993.

[5] Figures culled from Jewish Virtual Library website at
http://www.jewishvirtuallibrary.org/jsource/Terrorism/usvictims.html.

[6] Detailed descriptions of Palestinian organizations, governance organs, and political factions are contained in CRS Report RL34074, *The Palestinians: Background and U.S. Relations*, by Jim Zanotti.

January 2009 (also known as Operation Cast Lead, which was launched by Israel in response to repeated rocket attacks by Hamas and other Palestinian militants) and despite ongoing restrictions (often termed the "blockade" or "closure regime") by Israel and Egypt on the flow of people and goods into and out of the territory.

By consolidating its control over Gaza and pursuing popular support through resistance to Israel, Hamas seeks to establish its indispensability to any Arab-Israeli political arrangement. Many analysts believe that Hamas hopes to leverage this indispensability into sole or shared leadership of the PA in both the West Bank and Gaza—either through a power-sharing arrangement with Abbas and his Fatah movement, or through presidential and legislative elections (which were supposed to take place in January 2010 under PA law, but have been postponed pending factional agreement on conditions for holding them)—and to gain membership in or somehow supplant the Fatah-dominated PLO, which remains internationally recognized as the legitimate representative of the Palestinian people. Fatah's political hegemony inside the occupied territories has been undermined by the inability of the Fatah-dominated PLO to co-opt or incorporate Hamas, which has proved more resistant than secular Palestinian factions to the PLO's inducements. Egyptian-mediated efforts to forge a PA power-sharing arrangement in the West Bank and Gaza between Hamas and its traditionally dominant rival faction, the secular nationalist Fatah movement, have stalled repeatedly.[7]

Hamas also has gained popularity among many Palestinians at Fatah's expense because of its reputation as a less corrupt provider of social services (funded by donations from Palestinians, other Arabs, and international charitable front groups) and because of the image it cultivates of unflinching resistance to Israeli occupation. Some Palestinians perceive that Hamas is more rooted in the experiences and attitudes of West Bankers and Gazans than Fatah. Most leaders from Fatah's historic core, including current PA President/PLO Chairman Mahmoud Abbas, spent decades in exile with Yasser Arafat's PLO in various Arab states. Although many from Hamas's top leadership, including political bureau chief Khaled Meshaal, also have lived in exile for 30-plus years, Hamas has maintained a strong presence within the Palestinian territories since its inception.

For additional information on Hamas's historical background and on U.S. policy regarding Hamas, see **Appendix A**.

Threats Hamas Poses

Many Israelis fear the potential long-term threat Hamas could pose to Israel's physical and psychological security if its rocket capabilities expand, if it gains an unchallenged foothold in the West Bank, and/or if it otherwise finds a way to regularly target civilians inside Israel again. Although damage from Palestinian suicide bombings in 1994-1997 and 2000-2008 is difficult to measure qualitatively, the bombings constituted a fearsome means of attack. In the aggregate, suicide bombing attacks by Palestinian militants killed approximately 700 Israelis (mostly civilians within Israel proper),[8] with Hamas directly responsible for more than 400 of these

---

[7] The only previous power-sharing arrangement between Hamas and Fatah, the Saudi Arabia-brokered Mecca Accord of February 2007, quickly deteriorated into factional fighting that led to Hamas's takeover of Gaza in June 2007 (see **Appendix A** and **Appendix B**).

[8] Suicide bombing figures culled from Israel Ministry of Foreign Affairs website at http://www.mfa.gov.il/MFA/ Terrorism-+Obstacle+to+Peace/Palestinian+terror+before+2000/
(continued...)

---

deaths.[9] Israel also fears that Iran, Syria, and possibly other actors in the region might use Hamas's proximity to Israel either to facilitate a coordinated multi-front military attack or to mobilize regional and international political pressure against Israel through the precipitation of crises and *causes célèbres*.[10]

The ability of Palestinians from the West Bank and Gaza to target civilians inside Israel (e.g., through suicide bombings) has been drastically reduced in the post-second intifada environment through heightened Israeli security measures. A system of tightly patrolled barriers and crossings limits access to Israel from both territories—in Gaza's case, almost completely. The system also includes the West Bank separation barrier[11] that some Israelis envision as demarcating a border between Israel and a future Palestinian state, even though it strays from the 1948-1967 armistice line, known as the "Green Line," in several places. Israeli military and intelligence operations within the West Bank—including various obstacles to and restrictions on Palestinians' freedom of movement (some of which are designed to protect Israeli settlers and settlements)—buttress the barrier system there.

Rockets and Smuggling Tunnels

In reaction to constraints on access to Israel, Hamas and other Palestinian militant groups in Gaza have increased their strategic reliance on firing rockets and mortars indiscriminately at Israeli targets.[12] Rocket fire and the threat of future rocket fire with greater geographical range precipitated Israel's Operation Cast Lead against targets in Gaza in December 2008.[13] The approximately 8,350 rockets and mortars fired by Palestinians since 2001[14] have killed at least 28 Israelis and wounded dozens,[15] while the persistent threat of rocket fire has had a broader negative psychological effect on Israelis living in targeted communities.[16]

(...continued)

Suicide%20and%20Other%20Bombing%20Attacks%20in%20Israel%20Since.

[9] See footnote 4.

[10] Examples of international pressure on Israel are the various convoys and flotillas, including the so-called "Gaza Freedom Flotilla" in May 2010, seeking to thwart the Israeli-Egyptian closure regime and to raise awareness of the humanitarian and economic situation in Gaza. For more information, see CRS Report R41275, *Israel's Blockade of Gaza, the Mavi Marmara Incident, and Its Aftermath*, by Carol Migdalovitz.

[11] The barrier is referred to in different ways by different groups and individuals that are often reflective of various political or national ideologies. Commonly used alternative names are the "security fence" (often used by Israeli sources) and the "apartheid wall" (favored by Palestinians), although neither appellation describes the barrier's physical nature completely accurately. In some places, the barrier is mainly concrete; in others, mainly chain-link and/or wire.

[12] Since 2001, Hamas and several other Palestinian terrorist groups based in the Gaza Strip have attacked communities in southern and coastal areas of Israel with thousands of indiscriminately fired rockets and mortars. During the second Palestinian intifada in 2001, Hamas militia members and others fired homemade mortars at Israeli settlements in the Gaza Strip and launched the first locally produced "Qassam" rockets, named after the early-20th Century militant leader Sheikh Izz al Din al Qassam. Teams of engineers, chemists, and machinists have improved the range and payload of the Qassam series rockets over time, and Israeli military raids have targeted several individuals and facilities associated with rocket research and production operations.

[13] Over the years, rockets have expanded in range beyond relatively small Israeli communities near the Gaza border, such as the town of Sderot (population est. 24,000), to the larger coastal cities of Ashqelon (population est.120,000) and Ashdod (population est. 200,000) and to the Negev city of Beersheva (population est. 185,000). Mid-range Grad-style rockets (thought to be smuggled into Gaza) that travel farther than Qassam rockets have been fired from Gaza by Hamas, Palestinian Islamic Jihad (Al Quds series) and the Popular Resistance Committees (Nasser series).

[14] Information provided by Israeli government to CRS, November 2010.

[15] "Q&A: Gaza conflict," *BBC News*, January 18, 2009, available at
(continued...)

Since the end of Operation Cast Lead, Hamas has permitted far fewer rockets to be fired from Gaza by its military wing and other Palestinian militant groups, perhaps because of a desire to avoid another large-scale Israeli attack. Nevertheless, analysts and Israeli officials say that Hamas continues to manufacture and stockpile hundreds, if not thousands, of "Qassam" rockets.[17] These rockets have limited ranges, and are generally made from household ingredients such as fertilizer, sugar, alcohol, fuel oil, pipes, and scrap metal. The raw materials are generally smuggled into Gaza—thus circumventing the Israeli-Egyptian closure regime—via tunnels under the Egyptian border.

Since Israel's disengagement from Gaza in 2005, Hamas has promoted a dramatic expansion of the network of smuggling tunnels connecting Gaza with Egypt's Sinai Peninsula. Under the closure regime aimed at undermining Hamas's control over the territory, the tunneling network has become Gaza's primary economic engine and mode of rearmament for militants. In addition to raw materials for Qassam rockets and other explosive devices, press and trade reports and Israeli officials allege that thousands of mortars and hundreds of longer-range rockets in Hamas's arsenal[18] (some of which may have been manufactured in Iran or China) have been smuggled into Gaza through the tunnels. As of the summer of 2010, one report said that these longer-range rockets could include dozens of 122-mm Grad or Grad-style rockets (sometimes known as Katyushas) and 230-mm Oghabs, and possibly some 50 modified 240-mm Fajr-3 rockets that could conceivably reach Tel Aviv or Israel's nuclear facilities in the Negev Desert near Dimona.[19] Hamas and other Palestinian militants also have reportedly received small arms and anti-aircraft and anti-tank weapons through the tunnels.[20]

(...continued)

http://news.bbc.co.uk/2/hi/middle_east/7818022.stm.

[16] For a comprehensive treatment of this subject, see Human Rights Watch, *Rockets from Gaza: Harm to Civilians from Palestinian Armed Groups' Rocket Attacks*, August 6, 2009, available at http://www.hrw.org/en/reports/2009/08/06/rockets-gaza-0.

[17] Information provided to CRS by Israeli government, November 2010.

[18] Ibid.

[19] Ian Siperco, "Shield of David: The Promise of Israeli National Missile Defense," *Middle East Policy*, Vol. 17, Issue 2, Summer 2010.

[20] See "Report: Egypt seizes anti-aircraft weapons bound for Gaza," *haaretz.com*, September 7, 2010.

Figure 2. Map of Approximate Rocket Ranges from Gaza

(for rockets possibly possessed by Hamas and other Palestinian militant groups)

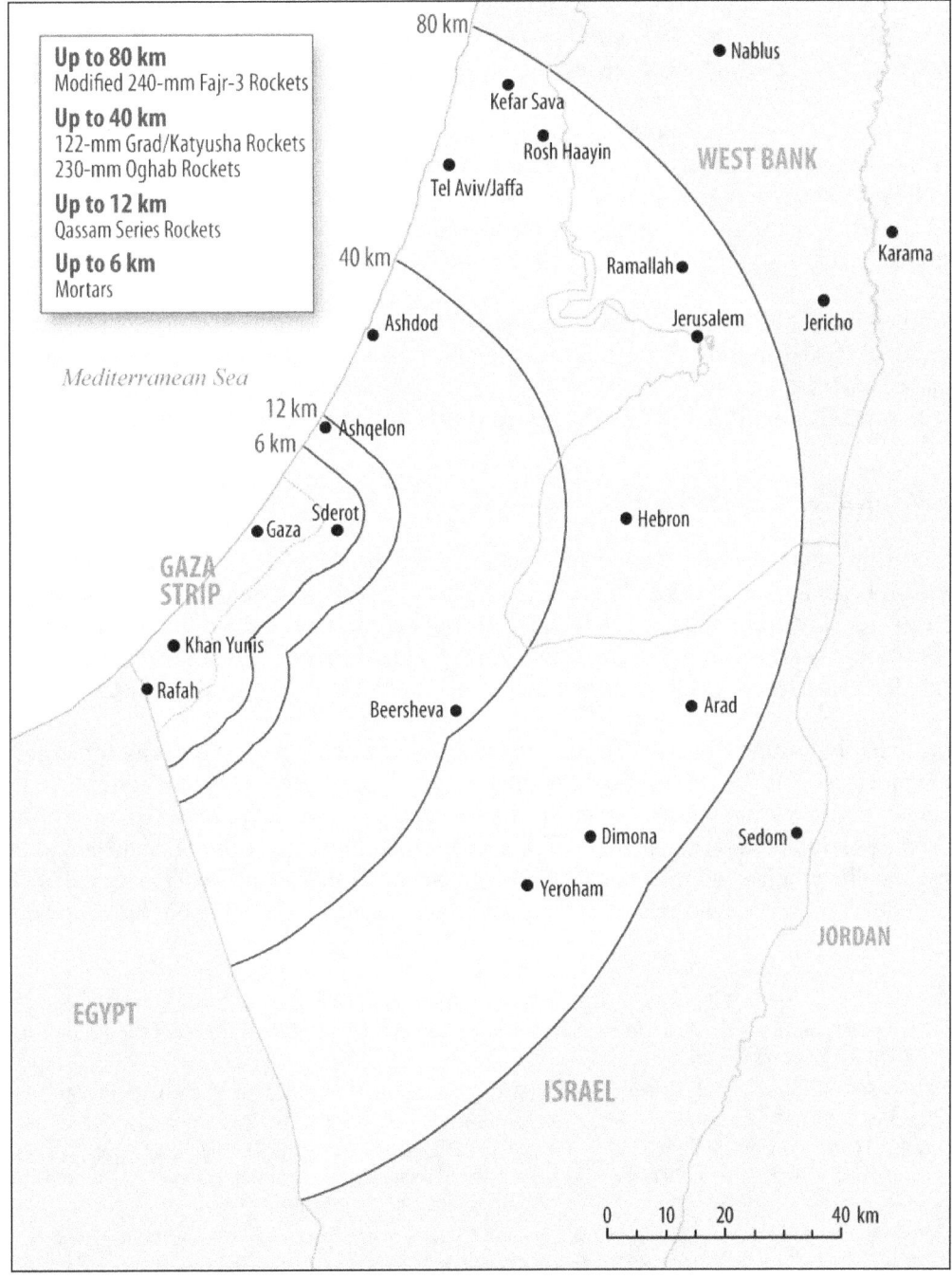

Sources: Congressional Research Service; *Jane's Missiles and Rockets*; Ian Siperco, "Shield of David: The Promise of Israeli National Missile Defense," *Middle East Policy*, Vol. 17, Issue 2, Summer 2010.

Notes: All boundaries, distances, and other depictions are approximate. The designations employed and the presentation of material on this map do not imply the expression of any opinion whatsoever on the part of CRS concerning the presence in Gaza of the rockets described herein. There is no evidence that rockets with a range farther than about 40 km have been fired at Israeli targets, though there have been reports that Hamas has successfully tested longer-range rockets.

Estimates say that approximately 7,000 people work on over 1,000 tunnels. The tunnels are reportedly of a generally high quality of engineering and construction—with some including electricity, ventilation, intercoms, and a rail system. The openings to many tunnels are found within buildings in or around Gaza's southernmost city of Rafah. Although Israeli airstrikes rendered over 100 tunnels inoperative during Operation Cast Lead, many of them were restored within a few weeks because the main damage was sustained at the openings, not in the middle sections.[21] Israel, Egypt, the United States, and other North Atlantic Treaty Organization (NATO) countries have pledged to stop or slow smuggling to Gaza by land and sea, and some measures such as Egypt's construction of an underground fence along its side of the Gaza-Egypt border (see "Countering Financial and Smuggling Networks") have been taken. Nevertheless, anti-smuggling capabilities remain limited and/or constrained.[22]

It also is possible that Hamas may have the capability to fire rockets from outside of Gaza. In August 2010, rockets fired from Egypt's Sinai Peninsula hit the neighboring cities of Eilat, Israel, and Aqaba, Jordan, on the Red Sea coast. Israeli and Egyptian officials, along with Palestinian Authority officials from the West Bank, claimed that Hamas was responsible.[23]

Gaza Militias and Security Forces

The leadership and most of the manpower—estimated at about 2,500—of Hamas's military wing, the Qassam Brigades, are in Gaza.[24] In addition, the Hamas-led government in Gaza maintains a robust contingent of approximately 13,000-14,000 police, security, and intelligence personnel, many of whom are drawn from the Executive Force that assisted the Qassam Brigades in defeating Fatah-led forces in Gaza in June 2007 (see **Table 3** and "In Gaza" below).[25]

It seems unlikely that the Qassam Brigades and Hamas-commanded Gaza security forces, even working in concert with other Gaza-based militants, could present a significant conventional threat to an Israeli military superior in manpower, equipment, and technology. Perhaps the main threat is the possibility that Hamas might kill or abduct additional Israeli soldiers to add to the leverage it believes it has gained against Israel with current Hamas captive Sergeant Gilad Shalit.[26] The Qassam Brigades and other militant groups engage in periodic border skirmishes

---

[21] Much of the information from this paragraph came from a CRS meeting with an Israeli official in August 2009. For a description of past smuggling activities related to Gaza, see CRS Report R40849, *Iran: Regional Perspectives and U.S. Policy*, coordinated by Casey L. Addis.

[22] See CRS Report RL33003, *Egypt: Background and U.S. Relations*, by Jeremy M. Sharp; and CRS Report RL34346, *The Egypt-Gaza Border and its Effect on Israeli-Egyptian Relations*, by Jeremy M. Sharp.

[23] "Netanyahu: Hamas responsible for rockets on Eilat; we will retaliate," *haaretz.com*, August 4, 2010; Anshel Pfeffer and Avi Issacharoff, "PA: Hamas military chief in Rafah ordered rocket attacks on Eilat, Aqaba," *haaretz.com*, August 6, 2010.

[24] Yezid Sayigh, *"We serve the people": Hamas policing in Gaza*, Crown Paper, Crown Center for Middle East Studies, Brandeis University, 2011 (forthcoming). This same source says that some of the security forces' personnel were holdovers from before the Hamas takeover. Some come from Fatah and other non-Hamas backgrounds.

[25] Mohammed Najib, "Hamas creates external intelligence arm," *Jane's Islamic Affairs Analyst*, January 29, 2010.

[26] Shalit, then a corporal, was taken captive in a June 2006 raid of an Israeli army post just outside Gaza. Two of Shalit's comrades were killed in the raid. The raid was organized jointly by the Popular Resistance Committees, Hamas, and an extremist jihadist group calling itself the Army of Islam. Shalit has remained in Hamas's custody since then, and his status figures prominently in speculation about negotiations with Hamas associated with a possible prisoner swap, cease-fire, or breakthrough in Palestinian power-sharing or Israeli-Palestinian negotiations. His well-being is a matter of major Israeli national concern.

---

with Israeli forces involving small arms and improvised explosive devices, partly to continually refresh their resistance credentials.

Hamas has portrayed its survival of Operation Cast Lead as a victory, but many analysts believe that Israel established some level of deterrence. These analysts say that Hamas did not expect the intensity of the Israeli operation and genuinely feared for the survival of its rule in Gaza. As a result, they suggest the group is now more cautious about possible provocations of Israel.[27]

Comparison with Other Middle East Terrorist Groups

Hamas is often discussed alongside other groups in the region that engage in militant and terrorist activities to achieve their ends. Israeli officials routinely compare Hamas with Al Qaeda. Yet Hamas has confined its militancy to Israel and the Palestinian territories—distinguishing it from the broader violent jihadist[28] aspirations expressed by Al Qaeda and its affiliates. This narrower focus was reflected by the following statement from Hamas political bureau (or politburo) chief Khaled Meshaal in a May 2010 interview with PBS's Charlie Rose:

> Hamas is a national resistance movement. Yet we adopt the Islamic intellectual approach because we are part of the Muslim and Arab region. We have a battle only with the Israeli occupation. We do not have any military act anywhere else in the world. We do not consider any country in the world other than Israel as our enemy. We might say that the American policies are wrong, but we do not have any conflict whatsoever except with the Israeli politics. In other words, we do not practice resistance as an open choice anywhere else in the world but in our occupied territories and against Israel. And we do not launch a religious war. We are not against the Jews nor the Christians. And we do not pass any statements about their religions. We only resist those who occupy our territories and attack us.[29]

Indeed, Al Qaeda voiced intense criticism of Hamas when it opted to engage in the Palestinian political process in 2005-2007 because its leaders believed Hamas was fatally compromising Al Qaeda's ideal of pan-Islamic revolution. Al Qaeda's number-two leader, Ayman al Zawahiri, said in 2006 that "Those trying to liberate the land of Islam through elections based on secular constitutions or on decisions to surrender Palestine to the Jews will not liberate a grain of sand of Palestine."[30]

---

[27] Yoram Cohen and Jeffrey White, *Hamas in Combat: The Military Performance of the Palestinian Islamic Resistance Movement*, Washington Institute for Near East Policy, Policy Focus #97, October 2009, available at http://www.washingtoninstitute.org/pubPDFs/PolicyFocus97.pdf.

[28] Jihadism is a concept with many different levels of meaning in Islam, from internal striving to external conflict between Muslims and non-Muslims (or sometimes between Muslims and other Muslims deemed to be insufficiently faithful). For more information, see CRS Report RS21695, *The Islamic Traditions of Wahhabism and Salafiyya*, by Christopher M. Blanchard.

[29] Transcript of remarks by Khaled Meshaal, "Charlie Rose," *PBS*, May 28, 2010, available at http://www.charlierose.com/view/interview/11032#frame_top. For additional information both supporting and countering Meshaal's statement above on Hamas's general stance toward Jews and Judaism, see "On Israel's Existence and the Jews" in the main body of the report.

[30] Beverley Milton-Edwards and Stephen Farrell, *Hamas: The Islamic Resistance Movement*, Polity Press, Malden, Massachusetts, 2010, p. 268. After Hamas agreed to a Saudi-brokered power-sharing arrangement with Fatah in February 2007 known as the Mecca Accord, Zawahiri claimed that "The leadership of Hamas government has committed an aggression against the rights of the Islamic nation by accepting what it called ... respecting international agreements. I am sorry to have to offer the Islamic nation my condolences for the [virtual demise] of the Hamas leadership as it has fallen in the quagmire of surrender." "Hamas rejects al-Zawahiri's claims," *aljazeera.net*, March (continued...)

Furthermore, hundreds of disaffected Palestinians in Gaza who apparently share Al Qaeda's misgivings that Hamas engages in unacceptable compromise have joined violent jihadist groups with Salafist[31] leanings or postures in opposition to Hamas. Nevertheless, Hamas has been willing to tolerate these smaller extremist groups to the extent they refrain from public challenges to Hamas's rule.[32] Hamas also coordinates action with others that reject peace with Israel—both Islamist and secular—under some circumstances.

Comparisons between Hamas and groups that blend political Islam with national or ethnic loyalties and grievances may be more apt. Hezbollah shares many characteristics with Hamas. It participates in electoral politics; it has a distinct geographical base of support; its main foreign backing comes from Iran. Perhaps most importantly, opposition to Israeli occupation or alleged occupation is a key animating factor for its supporters. Yet, significant differences exist between the two organizations, many of them following from Hezbollah's Shiite identity and greater freedom to traverse national borders. Shiites (Hezbollah's core demographic support base) constitute a significantly lower percentage of the population in Lebanon than the percentage Sunnis constitute in the Palestinian territories. Hezbollah's ties with Shiite Iran also are closer and more ideological than Hamas's. Hezbollah operatives actively train other militants (including from Hamas—see "Iran, Syria, and Hezbollah" below). Also, Hezbollah's rockets, other weapons, and militias are believed to present a significantly greater conventional military threat to Israel than Hamas's.[33]

Table I. Hamas and Hezbollah: A Comparison

	Hamas	Hezbollah
Established	1987	1982
National Identity	Palestinian	Lebanese
Sectarian Identity	Sunni Muslim	Shiite Muslim
Estimated Percentage of National Population That Shares Sectarian Identity	99%	28%-49%a
Named Foreign Terrorist Organization by State Department	1997	1997
Major Sources of Assistance	Iran, Syria, Hezbollah, private individuals and organizations	Iran, Syria, private individuals and organizations

(...continued)

12, 2007.

[31] Salafism refers to a broad subset of Sunni revivalist movements that seek to purify contemporary Islamic religious practices and societies by encouraging the application of practices and views associated with the earliest days of the Islamic faith. The world's Salafist movements hold a range of positions on political, social, and theological questions and include both politically quietist and violent extremist groups. Salafists generally eschew accommodation of "un-Islamic" political mechanisms such as Western-style democracy. For more information, see CRS Report RS21695, *The Islamic Traditions of Wahhabism and Salafiyya*, by Christopher M. Blanchard.

[32] Hamas took swift and brutal retributive action against the Army of Islam in September 2008 (in Gaza City) and Jund Ansar Allah in August 2009 (in Rafah) when confronted with challenges to its authority. Nicolas Pelham and Max Rodenbeck, "Which Way for Hamas?", *New York Review of Books*, November 5, 2009, available at http://www.nybooks.com/articles/archives/2009/nov/05/which-way-for-hamas/.

[33] For more information on Hezbollah and the threats it potentially poses, see CRS Report R41446, *Hezbollah: Background and Issues for Congress*, by Casey L. Addis and Christopher M. Blanchard.

	Hamas	Hezbollah
Members of National Legislature	74 of 132[b]	10 of 128
Ministers in National Government	All ministers in de facto Gaza government; no ministers in PA government in West Bank	2 of 30 (Agriculture and Administrative Reform); part of "March 8" coalition that has 10 ministers total
Estimated Troop Strength	2,500 in Qassam Brigades (military wing) 13,000-14,000 (some non-Hamas) in Gaza security forces	A few hundred terrorist operatives and potentially thousands more volunteers for defensive operations
Approximate Maximum Rocket/Missile Range	80 km	Over 100 km (and possibly over 200 km)
Territorial Control	Gaza Strip (using de facto control of national institutions and mechanisms)	Areas of southern and eastern Lebanon
Probable Main Weapon Supply Route	Tunnels under patrolled and fenced Gaza-Egypt border (14 km)	Loosely patrolled and unfenced Lebanon-Syria border (260 km)
Trains Militants of Other Nationalities	No evidence	Yes
Has Intentionally Struck at U.S. Targets in Middle East	Says no[c]	Yes

Sources: CRS Report R41446, *Hezbollah: Background and Issues for Congress*, by Casey L. Addis and Christopher M. Blanchard; Central Intelligence Agency; State Department; Council on Foreign Relations; Yezid Sayigh; International Foundation for Electoral Systems.

Notes: This comparison is not meant to be exhaustive.

a. U.S. State Department, International Religious Freedom Report 2009, available at http://www.state.gov/g/drl/rls/irf/2009/127352.htm; Pew Forum for Religion & Public Life, *Mapping the Global Muslim Population*, October 2009, available at http://pewforum.org/uploadedfiles/Orphan_Migrated_Content/Muslimpopulation.pdf. Because parity among confessional groups in Lebanon remains a sensitive issue, a national census has not been conducted since 1932.

b. Hamas won this legislative majority in 2006, but the Palestinian Legislative Council (PLC) has not been functional since Hamas's takeover of Gaza in June 2007 due to a lack of a quorum caused by the territorial political divide between Gaza and the West Bank. Furthermore, the PLC's four-year term expired in January 2010 under PA law, although the PLO Central Council extended its term in December 2009 (along with the PA presidential term of Mahmoud Abbas, which also expired in January 2010 under PA law) until new elections can be held. The legality of this extension has been questioned. For further information, see CRS Report RL34074, *The Palestinians: Background and U.S. Relations*, by Jim Zanotti.

c. Hamas has not claimed responsibility for any attacks targeting Americans, and insists that it targets only Israelis, but has killed at least 25 U.S. citizens (some of whom were dual U.S.-Israeli citizens) in attacks aimed at Israelis.

Hamas retains its claim to an electoral mandate because the majority it won in the Palestinian Legislative Council (PLC) in 2006 elections has not been displaced through subsequent elections (some say mainly due to reluctance by both Hamas and Fatah to risk their respective spheres of control in Gaza and the West Bank because of uncertainty regarding Palestinians' political preferences and factional advantages). As a result, many Hamas leaders, followers, and sympathizers identify the movement with other Sunni-led, Islamist-influenced groups and parties in the region that participate non-violently in their respective political arenas. These include Turkey's ruling Justice and Development Party (AKP) and non-militant branches and affiliates of the Muslim Brotherhood. Hamas's model of having a foot in both political and military realms serves as inspiration for other regional Islamist groups. This leads to concerns among regional states and the broader international community that Islamist groups elsewhere that participate or seek to participate non-violently in the political arena could turn to violence.

Ideology and Policies

Hamas combines Palestinian nationalism with Islamic fundamentalism, although opinions differ about how these two driving forces interact in Hamas's ideology and policies.[34] Its leaders strive to connect Hamas to the longer narrative of Palestinian national struggle—dating to the time of the British Mandate—and to past leaders such as the anti-colonialist Izz al Din al Qassam (see footnote 3), Mohammed Amin al Husseini (the Grand Mufti of Jerusalem during the British Mandate), and Abd al Qader al Husseini (a political and military leader who died in the 1948 war with Israel).

Some analysts insist that Hamas's actions show that it remains best defined by reference to its 1988 founding charter or "covenant," which sets forth a particularly militant, uncompromising, and anti-Semitic agenda.[35] These observers maintain this view despite and perhaps because of statements and documents issued over subsequent years by Hamas leaders purporting to redefine the movement's agenda or distance it from the charter, but failing formally to disavow it.[36]

Other analysts see Hamas as a pragmatic, evolving movement.[37] They argue that Hamas has already moderated its positions by participating in 2006 elections for the Palestinian Legislative Council, agreeing to short-term cease-fires with Israel through indirect negotiation, and expressing willingness to enter into a long-term cease-fire (or *hudna*) with Israel. Also, these observers say, Hamas signed the Mecca Accord in February 2007, pursuant to which it agreed to share power with Fatah, "respect" previous agreements signed by the PLO, and allow the PLO to negotiate with Israel and submit any agreement reached to the Palestinian people for their approval. Finally, these observers liken Hamas to the PLO from earlier times. The PLO, also once a terrorist group, altered some of its tenets in the late 1980s and early 1990s—agreeing to eschew violence, enter into negotiations with Israel (under the "land-for-peace" rubric of U.N. Security Council Resolutions 242 and 338), and recognize its right to exist.[38]

Still other analysts do not assume that Hamas remains committed to every word of its charter, but maintain that a decisive majority of Hamas members are unwilling to deviate from core principles

---

[34] See Matthew Levitt, "Political Hardball Within Hamas: Hardline Militants Calling Shots in Gaza," Washington Institute for Near East Policy, PolicyWatch #1450, January 6, 2009, available at http://www.washingtoninstitute.org/templateC05.php?CID=2982. This article contends that debate is most contentious within Hamas over which of these two driving forces to prioritize.

[35] See, e.g., Michael Herzog, "Can Hamas Be Tamed?", *Foreign Affairs*, March/April 2006; Charles Krauthammer, "Moral Clarity in Gaza," *Washington Post*, January 2, 2009.

[36] Many of these documents written subsequent to the Hamas charter can be found in Azzam Tamimi, *Hamas: A History from Within*, Olive Branch Press, Northampton, Massachusetts, 2007, Appendices. However, Fatah, whose leaders populate the main leadership positions of the PA and the PLO (which have dealings with Israel and the West), has not purged its 1960s charter of its clauses calling for the destruction of the Zionist state and its economic, political, military, and cultural supports (even though the PLO has recognized Israel's right to exist).

[37] See Henry Siegman, "US Hamas policy blocks Middle East peace," Norwegian Peacebuilding Centre, September 2010, available at http://www.usmep.us/usmep/wp-content/uploads/NorefReport_Siegman_Hamas-Israel_Sep10.pdf; Michael Bröning, "Hamas 2.0," *foreignaffairs.com*, August 5, 2009.

[38] See footnote 131.

---

of the movement—namely, its ability to resort to violence and its unwillingness to agree to a permanent peace or territorial compromise with Israel.[39] These analysts readily say that Hamas is not monolithic. Yet, they assert that in the instances in which Hamas conveys an impression of its pragmatism or potential moderation, consensus exists among its various political and military leadership bodies and councils that such actions are tactical, confined within the limits its core principles allow, and only bind Hamas as long as circumstances favor a diplomatic approach over a more confrontational one. Under this interpretation, statements from Hamas leaders hinting at permanent compromise of its core principles would either be deceptive or represent a marginalized view. For example, these analysts claim, Hamas's stated willingness to contemplate a long-term cease-fire in the event of the establishment of a Palestinian state in the West Bank (including East Jerusalem) and Gaza would allow Hamas to consolidate its position and await a more propitious moment to assault Israeli targets.[40]

Overall Goals

Hamas's primary goal is to achieve the "liberation" of all of historic Palestine (comprising present-day Israel, West Bank, and Gaza Strip) for Palestinian Arabs in the name of Islam. There is vigorous debate among analysts and perhaps within Hamas regarding the essential aspects of this goal. Hamas's charter is explicit about the struggle for Palestine being a religious obligation. It describes the land as a *waqf*, or religious endowment, saying that no one can "abandon it or part of it."

Those who believe that Hamas is pragmatic are less likely to believe that it considers itself bound by its charter or by rhetoric intended to rally domestic support. On the other hand, those who contend that consensus exists within Hamas not to compromise on core principles believe that Hamas sees events from a different perspective than U.S. and other international analysts. They assert that Hamas has a much different concept of time, borne out by a gradual but consistent rise in the movement's fortunes over the course of generations (within its greater Muslim Brotherhood context) in the face of significant internal challenges and external opposition.

On Israel's Existence and the Jews

The 1988 charter commits Hamas to the destruction of Israel and the establishment of an Islamic state in all of historic Palestine.[41] It calls for the elimination of Israel and Jews from Islamic holy land and portrays Jews in decidedly negative terms, citing anti-Semitic texts and conspiracies.

Many observers claim that subsequent statements from Hamas have refrained from or deemphasized blanket negative references to Jews and supposed global Zionist conspiracies. Some might say, however, that this is belied by numerous anti-Semitic statements and references

---

[39] CRS interview in September 2010 with U.S. analyst covering Middle East terrorism at major Washington, DC think tank.

[40] See Matthew Levitt, "Score One for 'Hamaswood,'" *Middle East Strategy at Harvard*, August 11, 2009, available at http://blogs.law.harvard.edu/mesh/2009/08/score-one-for-hamaswood/.

[41] For a translation of the 1988 Hamas charter (from the original Arabic), see http://avalon.law.yale.edu/20th_century/hamas.asp.

to pejorative stereotypes in media controlled by Hamas, including programming for both children and adults on Hamas's Al Aqsa satellite television channel.[42]

On a Two-State Solution

Although Hamas's charter is uncompromising in its call for the liberation of all of historic Palestine, those observers who contend that Hamas is essentially pragmatic point to past statements in which leaders pledged hypothetically to respect actions taken through a potential Palestinian referendum or PA power-sharing government (that includes Hamas) to accept a two-state solution.[43] Hamas politburo chief Khaled Meshaal, however, in an August 2010 interview, said:

> Hamas does accept a Palestinian state on the lines of 1967—and does not accept the two-state solution. There is [a] big difference between these two. I am a Palestinian. I am a Palestinian leader. I am concerned with accomplishing what the Palestinian people are looking for—which is to get rid of the occupation, attain liberation and freedom, and establish the Palestinian state on the lines of 1967. Talking about Israel is not relevant to me—I am not concerned about it. It is an occupying state, and I am the victim. I am the victim of the occupation; I am not concerned with giving legitimacy to this occupying country. The international community can deal with this (Israeli) state; I am concerned with the Palestinian people. I am as a Palestinian concerned with establishing the Palestinian state only.[44]

In a May 2010 interview with PBS's Charlie Rose, Meshaal clarified the circumstances under which Hamas would respect the outcome of a Palestinian referendum on the relationship with Israel held *after*, not before or concurrently with, the establishment of a Palestinian state:

> If Israel withdraws to the borders of 1967, and from East Jerusalem, that will become the capital of the Palestinian state with the right of self—with the right of return for the refugees and with a Palestinian state with real sovereignty on the land and on the borders and on the checkpoints. Then we—the Palestinian state will decide the future of the relationship with Israel. And we will respect the decision that will reflect the viewpoint of the majority of the Palestinian people.... Don't request the Palestinian people to have a certain stance from Israel while living under the Israeli occupation. Give the Palestinian people the opportunity to live in a normal situation in a Palestinian state, and then the Palestinian people with complete freedom will decide.[45]

---

[42] Matthew Levitt, "Hamas's Ideological Crisis," *Current Trends in Islamist Ideology Vol. 9*, Hudson Institute Center of Islam, Democracy, and the Future of the Muslim World, November 6, 2009, available at http://www.currenttrends.org/research/detail/hamass-ideological-crisis.

[43] Steven Erlanger, "Academics View Differences Within Hamas," *New York Times*, January 29, 2006.

[44] Sharmine Narwani, "Khaled Meshaal Interview: Hamas Chief Weighs In on Eve of Peace Talks," *The Huffington Post*, August 31, 2010.

[45] Transcript of remarks by Khaled Meshaal, "Charlie Rose," op. cit.

On the Use of Violence

Hamas's 1988 charter says, "There is no solution for the Palestinian question except through Jihad. Initiatives, proposals and international conferences are all a waste of time and vain endeavors."[46]

In the years since, the movement's willingness to halt violence and emphasize political over military methods in some circumstances, most notably the decision to participate in the 2006 PLC elections, has prompted some analysts to express hope that it might contemplate demilitarizing. Nevertheless, Hamas's leadership and many other analysts insist that no matter what other means Hamas may tactically employ from time to time, armed resistance remains its ultimate trump card.

In a July 2010 interview with the Jordanian newspaper *Al Sabeel*, Meshaal discussed how having the option to use violence enhances Hamas's ability to negotiate, in contrast to the lack of leverage he said the PLO has had since renouncing violence:

> The [PLO] negotiators say: "Negotiation is the option, the course and the only plan." They coordinate security with the enemy and implement the "Road Map" and its security requirements freely, with Israel offering nothing in return. What is there to force Olmert or Netanyahu to grant the Palestinians anything?
>
> Negotiation in the [PLO] case is out of its objective context; it is, merely from the perspective of political logic, lacking resistance and not based on the necessary power balance. The Vietnamese—for instance—negotiated with the Americans as the latter were retreating; thus negotiations were useful for turning the last page on American occupation and aggression. You are successful in negotiation and in imposing your conditions on the enemy depending on the number of power cards you have on the ground.[47]

On Its Model for an Islamic State

Hamas's charter envisions that Palestine will become an Islamic society that allows for coexistence of all religions "under its wing":

> The Islamic Resistance Movement is a distinguished Palestinian movement, whose allegiance is to Allah, and whose way of life is Islam. It strives to raise the banner of Allah over every inch of Palestine, for under the wing of Islam followers of all religions can coexist in security and safety where their lives, possessions and rights are concerned. In the absence of Islam, strife will be rife, oppression spreads, evil prevails and schisms and wars will break out.[48]

However, by reshaping PA institutions, laws, and norms to fit its ends—instead of fully overhauling them—and by allowing the U.N. Relief and Works Agency for Palestine Refugees in the Near East (UNRWA) and other international and non-governmental organizations to operate

---

[46] 1988 Hamas charter, op. cit.

[47] Translation (from the original Arabic) of *Al Sabeel* (Jordan) newspaper interview with Khaled Meshaal, available at http://www.middleeastmonitor.org.uk/articles/middle-east/1491-khaled-meshal-lays-out-new-hamas-policy-direction.

[48] 1988 Hamas charter, op. cit.

in Gaza, Hamas has opted—for the time being at least—for stability over a comprehensive societal transformation. Hamas interior minister Fathi Hamad has insisted:

> Claims that we are trying to establish an Islamic state are false. Hamas is not the Taliban. It is not al-Qaeda. It is an enlightened, moderate Islamic movement.[49]

Some ideologues who believed that Hamas would or should have implemented *sharia* law and formally and fully Islamized public and private life soon after taking power have been disappointed. This disappointment has resulted in some Islamists joining more extremist groups, though it does not appear to present a near-term challenge to Hamas's rule and it is unclear how pronounced or significant this trend will be long term.

Yet, there has been some movement toward a greater Islamization of society through the broader Hamas community network of mosques, reconciliation committees, government ministries and courts, security forces, religious scholars, and schools. Islamic *fatwas* (legal opinions) have been offered as an alternative to secular justice for some police detainees. "Morality police," judges, and school principals advocate for and enforce Islamic dress codes—especially for women—in publicly conspicuous places, although resistance to these measures has slowed or reversed their implementation in some instances.[50] How this has affected the minority of Palestinian Christians in Gaza is unclear. In February 2010, interior minister Fathi Hamad (in a statement that some could interpret as contradicting his above-quoted statement regarding Hamas's supposed moderation) "called for '*Da'wa* efforts to reach all institutions, not just mosques,' signaling an intent to systematically Islamize government agencies, starting with his own."[51]

Use of Media

Hamas has used its control over Gaza's media and a robust Internet presence[52] to cast Islamist, anti-Israel, and anti-Semitic teachings within a narrative portraying "martyrdom" and violence against Israel and Jews as heroic. Public dissent is suppressed, and Hamas uses its Al Aqsa television and radio channels and summer camps[53] to indoctrinate children and youth with its hybrid Islamist/Palestinian nationalist views. In 2009, Hamas even produced its first feature-length film celebrating the life and death of a Qassam Brigades militant from the first intifada.[54] It

---

[49] Pelham and Rodenbeck, op. cit..

[50] Ibid.

[51] Yezid Sayigh, "Hamas Rule in Gaza: Three Years On," Crown Center of Middle East Studies, Brandeis University, March 2010, available at http://www.brandeis.edu/crown/publications/meb/MEB41.pdf.

[52] Sayigh, *"We serve the people"*..., op. cit. For example, the Qassam Brigades (www.qassam.ps) and Al Aqsa TV (www.aqsatv.ps/ar/) maintain their own websites, and most (if not all) of the Hamas-run Gaza ministries, including the Ministry of Interior (http://www.moi.gov.ps), also maintain websites. Some of these websites have English and other foreign-language versions as well as Arabic.

[53] In May and June 2010, two separate incidents of arson were reported against Gaza summer camps run by UNRWA (that served approximately 250,000 Gaza youth in Summer 2010). Some analysts in Israel and the West believe that the incidents may have taken place with the tacit or express approval of Hamas in an attempt to promote its model for influencing youth over UNRWA's (Hamas's camps reportedly served approximately 100,000 Gaza youth in Summer 2010), given the criticism Hamas has reportedly leveled at the UNRWA camps for their focus on entertainment and potentially "corrupting" influences. See "This year Hamas' summer camps in the Gaza Strip…," Meir Amit Intelligence and Terrorism Information Center, September 14, 2010, available at http://www.terrorism-info.org.il/malam_multimedia/English/eng_n/html/hamas_e128.htm; Sarah A. Topol, "Hamas's Summer Camp War," *Slate.com*, July 27, 2010.

[54] Levitt, "Hamas's Ideological Crisis," op. cit.

---

encourages support and often recruits from "mosque youth" who assist neighborhood imams and sometimes act as informants for Hamas-controlled Gaza intelligence organizations.[55]

Hamas leaders also skillfully use regional and international media outlets to craft messages to its various audiences, including Arabs and Muslims, Americans, Europeans, and Israelis. Israeli officials insist that Hamas delivers the same message to Arab and Western audiences with a different tone and emphasis for each,[56] creating what some might call purposeful and convenient ambiguity over questions such as Hamas's possible pragmatism.

Leadership and Organization

In General

Hamas has a variety of movement-wide and regional leadership organs, along with branches that conduct its political, military, and social welfare activities with varying levels of formal association to the group. In addition, the de facto Hamas government in Gaza has its own leadership structures and public stature. Who controls overall strategy, policy, and financial decisions, and how control is exercised, remain open questions with opaque answers. The State Department and some analysts believe that Hamas generally follows a hierarchical model in which ultimate control resides with the 15-member political bureau (or politburo) and the movement-wide consultative council (known as the *shura* council) headquartered in Damascus.[57] According to Matthew Levitt of the Washington Institute for Near East Policy, "Under this Shura council are committees responsible for supervising a wide array of activities, from media relations to military operations. At the grassroots level in the West Bank and Gaza, local Shura committees answer to the overarching Shura council and carry out its decisions on the ground."[58] One reason to believe that substantial authority resides with the movement-wide and regional *shura* councils is that Hamas closely guards the secrecy of these councils' membership. Hamas also maintains branch offices in areas where it enjoys support, such as Lebanon, Sudan, the Gulf, and possibly Iran.[59]

Some analysts, however, believe that Hamas's formal hierarchical structures remain subject to a dispersion of control given that the geographical division of the organization's core activities among Damascus and Gaza—maintained out of necessity for the organization's security and survival—creates a system of mutual leverage. This system is based on how the actions and funding streams of Hamas's political, military, and social welfare branches affect their interactions, as these interactions both shape and are shaped by events.

Hamas seeks to mitigate the tension inherent between its activities as (1) a militant organization uncompromisingly opposed to Israel in defiance of international opprobrium and countermeasures; and (2) the de facto government in Gaza accountable to its people for managing

---

[55] Sayigh, *"We serve the people"...*, op. cit.

[56] Israel Defense Forces Intelligence, "The forked tongue of Hamas: How it speaks differently to Western and Arab media," April 11, 2006, available at http://www.mfa.gov.il/MFA/Terrorism-+Obstacle+to+Peace/Terror+Groups/The%20forked%20tongue%20of%20Hamas%2011-Apr-2006

[57] See U.S. State Department, "Country Reports on Terrorism 2009," Chapter 6, op. cit.

[58] Levitt, "Political Hardball Within Hamas...," op. cit.

[59] See Cohen and White, op. cit.

security, economic, and other basic societal issues that largely depend upon Israeli and international actions. Some might express this as Hamas's desire to maximize its power while minimizing its accountability. Hamas claims it draws a bright line bifurcating the organization's leadership from its members in the Gaza government, which, if true, helps it deflect accountability. This could discourage the United States and other international actors from including Hamas in political discussions tied to Palestinian governance or negotiations with Israel.

Internal Tensions?

Various U.S. and international policymakers, including Secretary of State Hillary Rodham Clinton, have said or implied that organizational fissures may exist within Hamas.[60] These possible fissures are somewhat overlapping. One supposedly runs between Gaza-based leaders accountable to local public opinion and Damascus-based leaders seen as closer to Iran. Another supposedly runs between so-called pragmatists and more hardline elements in the Gaza leadership (often Qassam Brigades militants and their sympathizers). Yet another is said to exist between two groups of Damascus exiles: (1) native Gazans with personal links to Hamas's Gaza founders (such as Musa Abu Marzouk), and (2) displaced West Bankers used to operating outside of the Palestinian territories who forged links with the Gaza founders mostly through Islamist organizations in Kuwait (known as *Kuwaitiyya*, this group includes Khaled Meshaal).

Within the Qassam Brigades, some analysts speculate that internal struggles may partly explain the rise of Jaljalat (an Arabic word for "thunder"), an "amorphous network of armed militants numbering some 2,500-3,000" that reportedly includes many disaffected Brigades members. Yezid Sayigh of King's College London, a longtime analyst of Palestinian security and politics and a former PLO advisor, claimed in a March 2010 report that Jaljalat fears that, "by taking on the mundane tasks of government and public service delivery, Hamas has jeopardized its nationalist and Islamic purity and its commitment to armed resistance against Israel." Sayigh's report also said that Jaljalat is suspected of several attacks on Hamas vehicles and security offices, as well as on Internet cafés. Additionally, the report said that Qassam Brigades commander Ahmed al Jaabari may be concerned that some Hamas leaders in Gaza may be building alternative power bases that could threaten the internal unity of Hamas and the Brigades.[61]

Hamas could be more united than it seems, although it benefits from the portrayal of its leadership as divided because this perception provides Hamas with greater flexibility in dealing with both Western actors who hold out hope of its moderation and its Syrian and Iranian benefactors who are reminded not to take its rejectionist stance for granted. Presenting a divided front also may serve Hamas by providing it with a rationale to explain policy inconsistencies or changes of direction to the Palestinian people.

---

[60] In testimony before the House Appropriations Subcommittee on State, Foreign Operations and Related Programs, Secretary of State Hillary Rodham Clinton said, "In fact, we think there is [sic] some divisions between the Hamas leadership in Gaza and in Damascus. There's no doubt that those in Damascus take orders directly from Tehran." Transcript of Subcommittee hearing: "Supplemental Request," April 23, 2009.

[61] The source for this paragraph is Sayigh, "Hamas Rule in Gaza: Three Years On," op. cit.

In Gaza

Hamas directs the Gaza government and security forces through a self-appointed cabinet of Hamas ministers led by Ismail Haniyeh, who served as PA prime minister prior to Hamas's dismissal from government after the June 2007 Gaza takeover. The process by which decisions are taken is opaque, but analysts believe that it involves the movement-wide and Gaza regional *shura* councils, the Damascus politburo, and Qassam Brigades leadership.[62] Along with an unknown amount it may receive from Hamas's organization and external benefactors, the Hamas-led government may receive revenue from Gaza's *zakat* committees (which collect Muslims' obligatory donations of 2.5% of their surplus wealth) and from licensing fees and taxes. Although Hamas is believed to make tens of millions of dollars annually from operating Gaza's smuggling tunnels (the estimate for 2009, according to Yezid Sayigh, was $150 million-$200 million), most of its profit reportedly goes to the organization (the Qassam Brigades, in particular), and not the Gaza regime.[63] The people of Gaza still rely on Israel, Egypt, the PA in the West Bank, UNRWA, and other international and non-governmental organizations for access to and resources from the outside world (including banking, water, and fuel for electricity).

Reference to the government in Gaza as the "Hamas regime" does not mean that all or even most of the people employed in ministries, civil service positions, and even security forces are necessarily members of Hamas or even Hamas sympathizers. Hamas partisans are, however, intermingled throughout. *The Jerusalem Report*, an Israeli weekly, states that since the June 2007 takeover, the PA in the West Bank has continued paying salaries to tens of thousands of public sector employees in Gaza—mostly in education- and health-related positions—while paying salaries to thousands more (including from the security forces) on the condition that they *not* perform their duties.[64] Although this policy might allow the PA to maintain the loyalties of its workers, it also has relieved the regime of the economic burden of supporting those paid by the PA. It also has given the regime the opportunity to create a critical mass of Hamas loyalists within the government by filling vacated positions in the security forces and other key public institutions. Additionally, the Hamas-led regime has created its own ad hoc judicial framework and hired its own judges,[65] many of them from *sharia* courts.[66]

---

[62] In a conversation with CRS in August 2009, an Israeli official claimed that the Damascus politburo, headed by Khaled Meshaal, exercises more strategic control over Hamas's activities than Hamas's other leadership organs because (the Israeli official claimed) the politburo is responsible for arranging the transport of cash, weapons, and other supplies to the Gaza Strip.

[63] CRS correspondence with Yezid Sayigh, October 2010.

[64] Danny Rubenstein, "Planet Gaza," *The Jerusalem Report*, June 7, 2010. U.S. appropriations legislation (including the Consolidated Appropriations Act, 2010 (P.L. 111-117)) prohibits U.S. aid to be "obligated for salaries of personnel of the Palestinian Authority located in Gaza." The U.S. Agency for International Development (USAID) says that direct U.S. budgetary assistance to the PA is used "to service debt to commercial suppliers and commercial banks." USAID FY2011 Congressional Notification #1, October 7, 2010.

[65] Nathan J. Brown, "Palestine: The Schism Deepens," Carnegie Endowment for International Peace, August 20, 2009, available at http://carnegieendowment.org/publications/index.cfm?fa=view&id=23668

[66] Sayigh, "Hamas Rule in Gaza: Three Years On," op. cit. *Sharia* courts seek the direct application of Islamic legal principles to society without reference to secular legal principles as possible supplements or alternatives.

Table 2. Public Budget Comparisons: Gaza and West Bank

	Gaza Hamas-led Regime	West Bank Palestinian Authority
Palestinian Population in Territory	1.55 million	2.04 million
Public Employees	32,000	145,000
Overall Annual Budget Estimates (2010)	$320 million-$540 million[a]	$2.78 billion
Annual Internal Revenue (2010)	$60 million	$1.54 billion
External Support Requirements (2010)	$260 million-$480 million	$1.24 billion

Sources: Central Intelligence Agency, State Department, Yezid Sayigh.

Notes: All figures are as of March 2010 and are approximate.

a. The Hamas-led regime in Gaza states that its 2010 budget is $540 million, but it is possible that the actual budget is closer to the actual budget for 2009, which was $320 million. CRS correspondence with Yezid Sayigh, October 2010.

Although much international attention has focused on the improved professionalization of PA security forces in the West Bank, analysts say that Hamas-led security forces in Gaza also exhibit impressive levels of discipline and efficiency that have succeeded in keeping order. There are, however, widespread reports of mistreatment and torture of Hamas political opponents (particularly Fatah members) and other prisoners; at the same time, similar reports circulate about PA treatment of Hamas members and sympathizers in the West Bank.[67]

Table 3. Major Hamas-commanded Security Forces in Gaza

Branch	Role	Estimated Manpower
Internal Security Service	Counterintelligence and infiltration of rivals (possibly including external intelligence arm)	500
VIP Protection Force	Bodyguards for Hamas leadership and key facilities	2,000
National Security Force	Border guard with early warning function	930
Police	Routine civil and criminal policing functions (largely derived from former "Executive Force")	10,000

Source: Mohammed Najib, "Hamas creates external intelligence arm," *Jane's Islamic Affairs Analyst*, January 29, 2010.

Many analysts believe that Hamas rule remains stable and effective in some areas despite the miserable post-Operation Cast Lead situation and Gaza's dilapidated infrastructure.[68] Some see the beginnings of a patronage system, citing, among other evidence, the $60 million in handouts

---

[67] See, e.g., Human Rights Watch, *Internal Fight: Palestinian Abuses in Gaza and the West Bank*, July 29, 2008, available at http://www.hrw.org/en/reports/2008/07/29/internal-fight-0.

[68] See, e.g., Daniel Byman, "How to Handle Hamas," *Foreign Affairs*, September/October 2010; Thanassis Cambanis, "Letter from Gaza," *foreignaffairs.com*, June 18, 2010.

Hamas is reported to have distributed in $1,500-$6,000 increments to families whose homes were lost or damaged in the conflict.[69] According to Yezid Sayigh, Hamas benefits from "unbroken territorial control over the entirety of the Gaza Strip." This stands in contrast to the difficulties faced by the Palestinian Authority in the West Bank, whose jurisdiction and operations are "fundamentally circumscribed by the 'Swiss cheese' model of intermeshed Palestinian autonomy areas and Israeli-controlled settlements and military zones."[70]

Popular Support

Although Hamas's rule in Gaza is authoritarian, it did win PLC elections in 2006, and some believe that the future possibility of elections makes it responsive to public opinion. Polls taken in the West Bank (including East Jerusalem) and Gaza Strip from August-October 2010 indicated that Palestinians favored Fatah over Hamas by nearly two-to-one to over three-to-one margins in each territory.[71] Large groupings of Palestinians (ranging in the various polls from 15% to nearly 40%), however, did not identify a factional preference,[72] possibly indicating popular malaise or cynicism regarding political developments and processes, or potential for volatility.

However, according to a September-October 2010 poll by the Palestinian Center for Policy and Survey Research, over 60% of Gazans (contrasted with just over 40% of West Bankers) supported both Hamas's August-September 2010 shooting attacks on Israeli settlers in the West Bank[73] and the idea of attacking civilians inside Israel.[74] Might the possible resumption by Hamas of regular attacks or other active opposition to Israeli-PLO negotiations gain it support from this demographic? In the same poll, Palestinians were almost evenly divided (those agreeing came out slightly ahead, by a 49%-48% margin) on the following question related to a possible two-state solution:

> There is a proposal that after the establishment of an independent Palestinian state and the settlement of all issues in dispute, including the refugees and Jerusalem issues, there will be a mutual recognition of Israel as the state of the Jewish people and Palestine as the state of the Palestinians people. Do you agree or disagree to this proposal?[75]

---

[69] "Country Report: Palestinian Territories," *Economist Intelligence Unit*, October 2009. Yet, some observers note that Hamas leaders have mostly avoided the type of conspicuous consumption in which many Fatah leaders have engaged since the 1990s, and which feeds widespread perceptions of corruption.

[70] Sayigh, "Hamas Rule in Gaza: Three Years On," op. cit.

[71] Palestinian Center for Policy and Survey Research, Palestinian Public Opinion Poll No. 37 (September 30-October 2, 2010), available at http://www.pcpsr.org/survey/polls/2010/p37e.html#table; Arab World for Research and Development, "Middle East Peace Process: Silver Linings Remain," August 8-14, 2010, available at http://www.awrad.org/pdfs/Oversample%20Results%20-%20Analysis%20%28final%29.pdf; Jerusalem Media and Communications Centre, Poll No. 71 (September 11-15, 2010), available at http://www.jmcc.org/documentsandmaps.aspx?id=808.

[72] Ibid.

[73] The shooting attacks, which coincided with the relaunch of Israel-PLO negotiations, killed four Israelis (including a pregnant mother) and injured two more.

[74] Palestinian Center for Policy and Survey Research, Palestinian Public Opinion Poll No. 37 (September 30-October 2, 2010), op. cit.

[75] Ibid.

Some reports indicate that Hamas is building its support base among Palestinian refugees outside of the West Bank and Gaza Strip, particularly in Lebanon.[76] Gaining the loyalty of refugee camp populations could give Hamas additional leverage with Fatah, Israel, and other regional actors.

Sources of Assistance

Iran, Syria, and Hezbollah

According to the State Department, Iran provides financial and military assistance to Hamas and other Palestinian militant groups.[77] During a December 2009 visit to Tehran, Hamas politburo chief Khaled Meshaal said, "Other Arab and Islamic states also support us ... but the Iranian backing is in the lead, and therefore we highly appreciate and thank Iran for this."[78] Meshaal and his politburo colleagues, along with Hamas's movement-wide *shura* council, have safe haven in Damascus, Syria. From Damascus, Hamas's leadership-in-exile can direct the group's operations through financial transactions and unrestrained access to travel and communications. The Iran-backed Hezbollah movement in Lebanon provides military training as well as financial and moral support and has acted in some ways as a mentor or role model for Hamas,[79] which has sought to emulate the Lebanese group's political and media success. Some Palestinians who are skeptical of the Arab-Israeli peace process believe that Iranian support for Palestinian militants and Hezbollah provides needed leverage with Israel that the United States and Europe are unlikely to deliver to PA President/PLO Chairman Mahmoud Abbas.

Some reports say that contributions to Hamas's political and military wings from Iran range from $20 million-$30 million annually.[80] Yet, even though Hamas welcomes direct and indirect Iranian assistance and Iran's reputation among Arab populations has arguably been bolstered in recent years by its anti-Western and anti-Israel positions and rhetoric, Hamas and Iran may intentionally maintain a measure of distance from one another. An alternate interpretation is that they merely understate the extent of their ties.[81] They appear to understand the importance of Hamas maintaining an image among its domestic constituents as an authentic Palestinian offshoot of the Muslim Brotherhood, instead of as an Iranian proxy—owing to the ethnic, sectarian, and

---

[76] See U.S. State Department, "Country Reports on Terrorism 2009," Chapter 6, op. cit.; International Crisis Group, *Nurturing Instability: Lebanon's Palestinian Refugee Camps*, Middle East Report No. 84, February 19, 2009, available at
http://www.crisisgroup.org/~/media/Files/Middle%20East%20North%20Africa/Israel%20Palestine/84%20nurturing%20instability%20lebanons%20palestinian%20refugee%20camps.ashx.

[77] See U.S. Department of State, "Country Reports on Terrorism 2009," Chapter 3. State Sponsors of Terrorism, available at http://www.state.gov/s/ct/rls/crt/2009/140889.htm.

[78] Transcript of remarks by Khaled Meshaal, *Al Jazeera TV*, December 15, 2009, Open Source Document GMP20091215648001 (translated from Arabic).

[79] Fitfield, op. cit; Thanassis Cambanis, *A Privilege to Die: Inside Hezbollah's Legions and Their Endless War Against Israel*, Free Press, New York, 2010, pp. 17, 267-272.

[80] See Council on Foreign Relations Backgrounder, "Hamas," updated August 27, 2009, available at http://www.cfr.org/publication/8968/#p8; Matthew Levitt, "The Real Connection Between Iran and Hamas," *Counterterrorism Blog*, January 12, 2009, available at http://counterterrorismblog.org/2009/01/the_real_connection_between_ir.php.

[81] See, e.g., Ehud Yaari, "Sunni Hamas and Shiite Iran Share a Common Political Theology," Washington Institute of Near East Policy, PolicyWatch #1716, November 9, 2010.

---

linguistic differences between Palestinians (who are predominantly Arab, Sunni, and Arabic-speaking) and Iranians (who are mostly non-Arab, Shiite, and Persian-speaking).

Iran's future influence over the Palestinian political scene seems tied to Hamas's fortunes, which have been on the rise since Hamas's political emergence in the late-1980s, and bolstered by its victory in Palestinian Legislative Council elections in 2006 and takeover of Gaza in 2007. Possible Iranian-supported smuggling of weapons, cash, and other contraband into the Gaza Strip,[82] along with Iranian training for Gaza-based Hamas militants (who are able to travel to and from Iran and Lebanon after using the Gaza-Sinai tunnels),[83] is believed to reinforce both Hamas's ability to maintain order and control over Gaza and its population, and Palestinian militants' ability to fire mortars and rockets into Israel.[84]

Charities and Individuals

U.S. officials and many analysts have concluded that, drawing upon its historical roots in and continuing ties to the Palestinian *dawa* (social welfare) community, Hamas receives much of its support from private individuals and organizations in the Palestinian diaspora and greater Arab and Muslim worlds (particularly in Saudi Arabia and other Gulf states).[85] Since 1995, the United States has taken active measures—in concert with Israel, the PA, and other international actors—to disrupt Hamas's use of charities as front organizations (see **Table 4** below and **Appendix A** for additional details).

Table 4. U.S. Terrorist Designations and Financial Sanctions Against Hamas and Affiliates

Hamas Designation	Statutory Basis	Financial Sanctions	Subject to Civil and/or Criminal Liabilitya
Specially Designated Terrorist (SDT) January 1995 Executive Order 12947	International Emergency Economic Powers Act (P.L. 95-223, 50 U.S.C. §1701, et seq.)	Blocks all U.S. property of SDT (or of party controlled by SDT or acting on its behalf)	Any transaction or dealing by a U.S. person or within the United States with SDT or SDT property

---

[82] Uzi Mahnaimi, "US navy seeks arms bound for Hamas," *The Sunday Times* (UK), January 25, 2009.

[83] Byman, op. cit.

[84] According to the State Department, in 2009, "Iran remained the principal supporter of groups that are implacably opposed to the Middle East Peace Process. The Qods Force, the external operations branch of the Islamic Revolutionary Guard Corps (IRGC), is the regime's primary mechanism for cultivating and supporting terrorists abroad. Iran provided weapons, training, and funding to HAMAS and other Palestinian terrorist groups, including Palestine Islamic Jihad (PIJ) and the Popular Front for the Liberation of Palestine-General Command (PFLP-GC)." U.S. Department of State, "Country Reports on Terrorism 2009," Chapter 3, op. cit. See also Marie Colvin, "Hamas Wages Iran's Proxy War on Israel," *The Sunday Times* (UK), March 9, 2008.

[85] See U.S. Treasury Department press release: "U.S. Designates Five Charities Funding Hamas and Six Senior Hamas Leaders as Terrorist Entities," August 22, 2003, available at http://www.ustreas.gov/press/releases/js672.htm; U.S. Treasury Department press release: "Treasury Designates Al-Salah Society Key Support Node for Hamas," August 7, 2007, available at http://www.treas.gov/press/releases/hp531.htm. See also Don Van Natta, Jr., with Timothy L. O'Brien, "Flow of Saudi Cash to Hamas Is Under Scrutiny by U.S.," *New York Times*, September 17, 2003.

Hamas Designation	Statutory Basis	Financial Sanctions	Subject to Civil and/or Criminal Liability[a]
Foreign Terrorist Organization (FTO) October 1997 State Department	Antiterrorism and Effective Death Penalty Act of 1996 (P.L. 104-132, 110 Stat. 1214-1319)	Requires financial institutions to block all funds in which FTOs or their agents have an interest	U.S. persons providing material support or resources to FTOs; failure of financial institutions to block funds
Specially Designated Global Terrorist (SDGT) October 2001 Treasury Department (Under Executive Order 13224)	International Emergency Economic Powers Act (P.L. 95-223, 50 U.S.C. §1701, et seq.)	Blocks all U.S. property of SDGT (or of party controlled by SDGT or acting on its behalf) and of those who provide material support to SDGT Directs executive branch to work with other countries to prevent acts of terrorism, deny financing to terrorists, and share intelligence about terrorist funding activities	Any transaction or dealing by a U.S. person or within the United States with SDGT or SDGT property

Source: U.S. Treasury Department, Office of Foreign Assets Control, "What You Need to Know About U.S. Sanctions," available at http://www.ustreas.gov/offices/enforcement/ofac/programs/terror/terror.pdf.

a.   See footnote 87 and footnote 88, respectively, for discussion of the statutory bases for U.S. criminal and civil liability for material support of terrorism (18 U.S.C. §2333, §2339A, §2339B).

Yet, it appears that, either through the international banking system or the Gaza-Sinai smuggling tunnels (or both), Hamas's political and military wings both still receive funding from their own networks of affiliated Islamic charities,[86] including some that have operated and may still operate in the United States, Canada, and Europe. The most illustrative case was that of the Texas-based Holy Land Foundation for Relief and Development (HLF), once the largest Islamic charity in the United States. After U.S. investigators determined that HLF was funneling money to Hamas and had close ties with Hamas leader Musa Abu Marzouk when he lived in the United States in the early 1990s, the Treasury Department named HLF a specially designated global terrorist (SDGT) in 2001 and froze its assets. In 2008, five HLF leaders (four of whom are U.S. citizens) were found guilty on criminal charges of providing more than $12 million in material support to Hamas (through contributions to Hamas-linked charities) after President Bill Clinton had named Hamas a specially designated terrorist (SDT) by executive order in 1995.[87] For providing financing, HLF and two affiliated organizations also were found liable in 2004 in federal civil court for the 1996 Hamas shooting death of an Israeli-American dual citizen in Jerusalem, although the verdict against HLF was reversed on appeal in 2007 on procedural grounds.[88]

---

[86] Matthew Levitt and Michael Jacobson, *The Money Trail: Finding, Following, and Freezing Terrorist Finances*, Washington Institute for Near East Policy, Policy Focus #89, November 2008, available at http://www.washingtoninstitute.org/pubPDFs/PolicyFocus89.pdf.

[87] See U.S. Department of Justice press release, Holy Land Foundation, Leaders, Accused of Providing Material Support to Hamas Terrorist Organization, July 27, 2004, available at http://www.justice.gov/opa/pr/2004/July/04_crm_514.htm. Criminal liability for material support of terrorism is authorized under 18 U.S.C. §2339A and §2339B. For further information, see CRS Report R41333, *Terrorist Material Support: An Overview of 18 U.S.C. 2339A and 2339B*, by Charles Doyle.

[88] Laura B. Rowe, "Ending Terrorism with Civil Remedies: Boim v. Holy Land Foundation and the Proper Framework of Liability," 4 Seventh Circuit Review 372 (2009), available at http://www.kentlaw.edu/7cr/v4-2/rowe.pdf. In addition (continued...)

The December 2004 findings of the Intelligence and Terrorism Information Center (an Israeli non-governmental organization), as paraphrased in a November 2008 Washington Institute for Near East Policy report, claimed that there were two separate categories of Hamas-linked charitable fronts:

> The first category includes those fronts directly tied to Hamas. These typically employ Hamas activists, are established with the assistance of the Hamas political leadership, and see the vast majority of their funds dispensed to Hamas charities in the West Bank and Gaza. Such charities bring in an estimated $15–$20 million a year and include the Palestinian Relief and Development Fund (Interpal) and the al-Aqsa International Foundation, among others. The second category includes fronts that support radical Islamist elements generally but are not Hamas specific. A majority of these fronts are based in Persian Gulf states and most of the funds they send to the West Bank and Gaza are also channeled through Hamas organizations there.[89]

In November 2008, the Treasury Department identified one of these alleged front organizations, a Saudi Arabia-based charity known as the Union of Good, as an SDGT, claiming that the organization had been responsible for the transfer of tens of millions of dollars to Hamas-managed associations in the Palestinian territories. The Union of Good is reportedly chaired by Yusuf al Qaradawi,[90] a renowned Egyptian scholar of Islam and Hamas supporter based in Qatar whose popular religious program on the Al Jazeera satellite television channel attracts approximately 40 million viewers. At the time of the Union's SDGT designation, the Treasury Department stated:

> The leadership of Hamas created the Union of Good in late-2000, shortly after the start of the second Intifada, in order to facilitate the transfer of funds to Hamas. The Union of Good acts as a broker for Hamas by facilitating financial transfers between a web of charitable organizations—including several organizations previously designated under E.O. 13224 for providing support to Hamas—and Hamas-controlled organizations in the West Bank and Gaza. The primary purpose of this activity is to strengthen Hamas' political and military position in the West Bank and Gaza, including by: (i) diverting charitable donations to support Hamas members and the families of terrorist operatives; and (ii) dispensing social welfare and other charitable services on behalf of Hamas.... [S]ome of the funds transferred by the Union of Good have compensated Hamas terrorists by providing payments to the families of suicide bombers.[91]

According to the Israel Security Agency (also known as the Shin Bet), several Islamic charitable organizations withdrew their funding from the Union of Good shortly after its SDGT designation.[92]

(...continued)

to other civil penalties that may accrue, civil liability for damages caused by a party's support of terrorism is authorized under 18 U.S.C. §2333, which states: "Any national of the United States injured in his or her person, property, or business by reason of an act of international terrorism ... may sue therefor ... and shall recover threefold the damages he or she sustains..."

[89] Levitt and Jacobson, op. cit., citing the Intelligence and Terrorism Information Center.

[90] Israel Security Agency (also known as the Shin Bet), "The Union of Good – Analysis and Mapping of Terror Funds Network," available at http://www.shabak.gov.il/SiteCollectionImages/english/TerrorInfo/coalition_en.pdf.

[91] U.S. Treasury Department press release HP-1267, "Treasury Designates the Union of Good," November 12, 2008, available at http://www.ustreas.gov/press/releases/hp1267.htm.

[92] Israel Security Agency, op. cit.

Some analysts believe that Hamas and other Palestinian militant groups may benefit from trade-based money laundering.[93] Charities, companies, and individuals purchase high-demand commodities like sugar, tea, coffee, and cooking oil to be sold in Palestinian areas because of the scarcity of these items under the Israeli-Egyptian closure regime. Orders can be worth hundreds of thousands of dollars.[94] Some groups, such as the Anti-Defamation League, have raised concerns over the participation of U.S. citizens and use of private U.S. funds in protest convoys (including the May 2010 *Mavi Marmara* flotilla discussed below—see "International Dimensions") directed at the Israeli-Egyptian closure regime that have raised money and donated supplies to Palestinians in Gaza, partly because of the difficulty in confirming that the recipients are not linked with Hamas. In July 2009, approximately 200 U.S. activists participated in a convoy organized by the British organization Viva Palestina (led by then British parliamentarian George Galloway) that entered Gaza from Egypt and donated approximately $500,000 worth of medical supplies (purchased from funds raised in the United States earlier in 2009) to Palestinian groups.[95]

Possible Options for Congress

In considering legislative and oversight options, Congress can assess how Hamas has emerged and adapted over time, and also scrutinize the track record of U.S., Israeli, and international policy to counter Hamas. There have been multiple attempts to marginalize Hamas through a variety of measures—political and foreign aid strategies, financial sanctions, arrests and deportations, physical blockades and border closures, and Israeli military operations and assassinations. Some of these measures have achieved temporary or partial success, but none has yet prevented Hamas from playing a major role in Israeli-Palestinian politics or prevented assistance to Hamas from states and other non-state actors in its region. Some might contend that U.S. policy with respect to Hamas since its initial U.S. terrorist designation in 1995 has strengthened instead of weakened the organization given its increased regional and international profile. Perhaps U.S. policy also has increased Hamas's reliance on the type of grassroots support that is not easily countered by governmental means. Others might say that the proper goal is to further strengthen the measures that have achieved temporary or partial success.

The following questions could be useful in evaluating legislative or oversight options:

- Is Hamas stronger than it was five years ago? 15 years ago? Why or why not? Have its rivals become stronger or weaker over that same period of time? (Strength could be measured by one of more of the following factors: popularity, military force, leverage with Israel, regional and global influence.)

---

[93] Glenn R. Simpson and Benoit Faucon, "A Trail of Sugar to Gaza," *Wall Street Journal*, July 2, 2007.

[94] For example, an allegedly suspicious 2005 food shipment to Gaza by the *Comité de Bienfaisance et de Secours aux Palestiniens*, a French organization the United States considers to be a Specially Designated Terrorist Organization due to its ties to Hamas, was worth $521,130. Simpson and Faucon, op. cit.

[95] Anti-Defamation League, "Viva Palestina: Supporting Hamas Under the Guise of Humanitarianism," July 22, 2009, available at http://www.adl.org/main_Anti_Israel/galloway_us_tour_09.htm?Multi_page_sections=sHeading_4. Concerns about possible links to Hamas may have been fueled by Galloway's actions during a previous European convoy's trip to Gaza in March 2009, when he gave approximately $1.5 million in cash and 110 vehicles directly to the Hamas-led regime.

- What are the United States' ultimate goals for Israel, the Palestinians, and the broader region? How do particular options regarding Hamas fit into these goals?

- What are Hamas's ultimate goals and how might Hamas act proactively to achieve these goals? How might it react to particular U.S. options that it perceives could serve or frustrate these goals?

- Once implemented, when are various options likely to produce results? What are U.S. capacities and political will for implementing and monitoring various options over time? What are intervening variables (i.e., other relevant actors, other issues that might distract from those addressed by various options, political timelines) and how might their potential negative impact on different options be minimized?

- How would the success of various options be measured?

U.S. Aid to Palestinians

Aid to Strengthen Non-Hamas Groups and Individuals

The current U.S. aid program for the West Bank-based PA led by President Mahmoud Abbas and Prime Minister Salam Fayyad dates back to June 2007. Since that time, U.S. bilateral assistance to the West Bank and Gaza Strip has amounted to approximately $2 billion, and assistance to UNRWA for Palestinian refugees (including in Gaza) has totaled over $700 million.[96]

This assistance includes $395.4 million (including $100 million in FY2010 funding) that have been appropriated or reprogrammed for use in the West Bank since 2007 to train, reform, advise, house, and provide non-lethal equipment for PA civil security forces in the West Bank loyal to President Abbas. A small amount of training assistance also has been provided to strengthen and reform the PA criminal justice sector. The Obama Administration has requested an additional $150 million in FY2011 funding for the security assistance program, which U.S. officials insist is only designed for West Bank security, and not for a prospective PA invasion of Hamas's stronghold in Gaza.

The current U.S. aid program appears to reflect a threefold strategy with respect to Hamas:

- First, humanitarian aid is provided to Gaza to provide the people with basic needs and to prevent destabilization.

- Second, assistance (budgetary, development, security) provided for the West Bank is intended to create a virtuous cycle of prosperity for Palestinians under Abbas's rule to contrast with the relative indigence of Gaza under Hamas, with the idea that Palestinians will reject the Hamas model and embrace the West Bank model.

- Third, the West Bank security assistance is largely intended to combat, neutralize, and prevent terrorism from Hamas and other militant organizations.

---

[96] For further information, see CRS Report RS22967, *U.S. Foreign Aid to the Palestinians*, by Jim Zanotti.

Reevaluations might focus on the prospects for these three strategies to achieve their purposes. Some analysts argue that improvements in Palestinians' material well-being brought about by the current aid program might be necessary, but are unlikely to be sufficient in achieving lasting support for non-Hamas political elements without more direct progress on (1) Hamas-Fatah power-sharing, (2) Palestinian political reform (including presidential and legislative elections), and/or (3) Israeli-Palestinian negotiations.[97] Nathan Brown of the Carnegie Endowment for International Peace, a longtime U.S. analyst of Palestinian politics, warned in June 2010 that the problem with "soldiering on" with the current strategy is that U.S. and Israeli policy inertia cedes the initiative to other actors:

> As has been shown time and again in recent years (most recently with the Gaza blockade), both Israel and the United States have unfortunately but unmistakably (and quite consistently) maintained policies until a crisis forces them to reevaluate....
>
> .... A political misstep by the West Bank government, an eruption of violence against Israeli targets originating either in the West Bank or Gaza, an upsurge in the conflict in Jerusalem, an extensive Israeli military campaign in Gaza, or the loss of one of the two indispensible men of the moment (Fayyad and Abbas) would likely leave both countries once more desperately rather than deliberately adjusting their policies toward internal Palestinian politics, and doing so most likely on unfavorable terms.[98]

Some analysts present U.S. involvement with Palestinian politics and institutions over the past 15 years as a cautionary tale,[99] stating or implying that the continuation of U.S. policies intended to present the West Bank as a model for Gazans to emulate might backfire—due either to negative outcomes or negative perceptions (or both).[100]

Some members of Congress advocate expanding the level and type of humanitarian and development assistance to Gaza—often at the same time they advocate easing, ending, or even challenging the Israeli-Egyptian closure regime—because Gazans are seen as needing more support to improve their economic, physical, and psychological situations.[101] Senator John Kerry, chairman of the Senate Foreign Relations Committee, and Representatives Brian Baird and Keith Ellison visited U.N. officials in Gaza in February 2009 (in the first official U.S. government visits to Gaza since 2003) to highlight Gazans' needs immediately following Operation Cast Lead. Representative Baird has since returned to Gaza twice, once in May 2009 with Representatives Donna Edwards and Peter Welch, and once in February 2010. In January 2010, 54 Representatives signed a letter to President Obama that requested a substantive lifting of the closure regime.[102]

---

[97] See, e.g., Nathan J. Brown, "Fayyad Is Not the Problem, but Fayyadism Is Not the Solution to Palestine's Political Crisis," op. cit.; Michele Dunne, "A Two-State Solution Requires Palestinian Politics," Carnegie Endowment for International Peace, June 2010, available at http://www.carnegieendowment.org/files/palestine_politics.pdf.

[98] Nathan J. Brown, "Are Palestinians Building a State?", Carnegie Endowment for International Peace Commentary, June 2010, available at http://www.carnegieendowment.org/files/palestinian_state1.pdf.

[99] See Dunne, op. cit.

[100] See, e.g., Mohammed Najib, "Struggling on – Khaled Mashal, political chief of Hamas," *Jane's Intelligence Weekly*, August 20, 2010.

[101] For further information on conditions in Gaza, see, e.g., Amnesty International UK, et al., "Dashed Hopes: Continuation of the Gaza Blockade," November 30, 2010, available at http://www.oxfam.org/sites/www.oxfam.org/files/dashed-hopes-continuation-gaza-blockade-301110-en.pdf; Sarah A. Topol, "'Gaza Is Not Darfur!'", *Slate.com*, August 5, 2010.

[102] Text of Letter to the President, January 20, 2010, available at
(continued...)

U.S. Security Assistance in the West Bank[103]

As mentioned above, the Bush and Obama Administrations have given non-lethal aid for PA civil security forces in the West Bank loyal to President Abbas in an effort both to counter militants from Hamas and other militants, and to establish the rule of law for an expected Palestinian state. This U.S. assistance program exists alongside other assistance and training programs reportedly provided to Palestinian security forces and intelligence organizations by the European Union and various countries, including probable covert U.S. assistance programs.[104] By most accounts, the PA forces receiving training have shown increased professionalism and have helped substantially improve law and order and lower the profile of terrorist organizations in West Bank cities.

However, the aspiration to coordinate international security assistance efforts and to consolidate the various PA security forces under unified civilian control that is accountable to rule of law and to human rights norms remains largely unfulfilled. PA forces have come under criticism for the political targeting of Hamas—in collaboration with Israel and the United States—through massive shutdowns and forced leadership changes to West Bank charities with alleged ties to Hamas members and through reportedly arbitrary detentions of Hamas members and supporters.[105] A September-October 2010 Palestinian Center for Policy and Survey Research poll indicated that 76% of Palestinians (with opinions nearly uniform between Gazans and West Bankers) opposed or strongly opposed the PA's mass arrests of Hamas members and sympathizers following Hamas's August-September 2010 shooting attacks against Israeli settlers in the West Bank.[106] Some Palestinians and outside observers also assert that the effectiveness and credibility of PA operations are undermined by Israeli restrictions—including curfews, checkpoints, no-go zones, and limitations on international arms and equipment transfers—as well as by Israel's own security operations in the West Bank[107] and the Gaza closure regime.

(...continued)

http://docs.google.com/viewer?url=http%3A%2F%2Fellison.house.gov%2Fimages%2Fstories%2FDocuments%2F2010%2FGaza_letter_to_Obama.pdf.

[103] For more information on this subject, see CRS Report R40664, *U.S. Security Assistance to the Palestinian Authority*, by Jim Zanotti; Government Accountability Office, Palestinian Authority: U.S. Assistance Is Training and Equipping Security Forces, but the Program Needs to Measure Progress and Is Facing Logistical Constraints, May 2010, available at http://www.gao.gov/new.items/d10505.pdf.

[104] See, e.g., Ian Cobain, "CIA working with Palestinian security agents," *guardian.co.uk*, December 17, 2009; Yezid Sayigh, "'Fixing Broken Windows': Security Sector Reform in Palestine, Lebanon and Yemen," Carnegie Endowment for International Peace, October 2009, available at http://www.carnegieendowment.org/files/security_sector_reform.pdf.

[105] See, e.g., Nathan Thrall, "Our Man in Palestine," *New York Review of Books*, October 14, 2010, available at http://www.nybooks.com/articles/archives/2010/oct/14/our-man-palestine/. For further discussion of human rights concerns surrounding PA security forces in the West Bank and Hamas in Gaza, see CRS Report R40664, *U.S. Security Assistance to the Palestinian Authority*, by Jim Zanotti; Human Rights Watch, *Internal Fight: Palestinian Abuses in Gaza and the West Bank*, op. cit.

[106] Palestinian Center for Policy and Survey Research, Palestinian Public Opinion Poll No. 37 (September 30-October 2, 2010), available at http://www.pcpsr.org/survey/polls/2010/p37e.html#table.

[107] See International Crisis Group, *Squaring the Circle: Palestinian Security Reform Under Occupation*, Middle East Report No. 98, September 7, 2010, available at http://www.crisisgroup.org/~/media/Files/Middle%20East%20North%20Africa/Israel%20Palestine/98%20Squaring%20the%20Circle%20--%20Palestinian%20Security%20Reform%20under%20Occupation.ashx; International Crisis Group, *Ruling Palestine II: The West Bank Model?* Middle East Report No. 79, July 17, 2008, available at http://www.crisisgroup.org/library/documents/middle_east___north_africa/arab_israeli_conflict/79_ruling_palestine_ii___the_west_bank_model.pdf. These operations underscore the fact that the Israeli-Palestinian agreements that authorized the creation of Palestinian security forces in the 1990s in areas of limited Palestinian self-rule contained (continued...)

United Nations Relief and Works Agency for Palestine Refugees in the Near East (UNRWA) in Gaza

The United States is the largest single-state donor to UNRWA, which provides food, shelter, medical care, and education for many of the original refugees from the 1948 Arab-Israeli war and their descendants—now comprising approximately 4.8 million Palestinians in Jordan, Syria, Lebanon, the West Bank, and Gaza.[108] Most observers acknowledge that the role of UNRWA in providing basic services (i.e., food, health care, education) in Gaza takes much of the governing burden off Hamas. As a result, some complain that this amounts to UNRWA's enabling of Hamas and is an argument militating for discontinuing or scaling back UNRWA's activities. However, many others, U.S. and Israeli officials included, believe that UNRWA plays a valuable role by providing stability and serving as the eyes and ears of the international community in Gaza. They generally prefer UNRWA to the uncertain alternative that might emerge if UNRWA were removed from the picture.[109]

Restrictions on Aid to Hamas or PA Government Including Hamas

Under current appropriations legislation, the United States cannot provide financial assistance to Hamas under any conditions. This law also prohibits U.S. assistance to a PA government with Hamas ministers unless all the government's ministers accept the "Section 620K principles": (1) recognition of "the Jewish state of Israel's right to exist" and (2) acceptance of previous Israeli-Palestinian agreements—named after the section in the Palestinian Anti-Terrorism Act of 2006 (P.L. 109-446) that sets them forth. These principles have some similarity to the principles the so-called international Quartet (United States, European Union, United Nations, and Russia) has required Hamas to meet before accepting dealings with it: (1) recognizing Israel's right to exist, (2) renouncing violence, and (3) accepting previous Israeli-Palestinian agreements. Hamas has alleged that the United States has used its leverage with Abbas to "veto" any serious attempt to broker a power-sharing compromise (by threatening an aid cutoff if Hamas rejoins the PA without accepting the Section 620K principles and/or Quartet principles), and some analysts understand the situation similarly.[110]

Future debates might focus on the following issues:

- Whether to relax or tighten U.S. restrictions on which Palestinian party/ies should be answerable for accepting and complying with the Section 620K principles.

(...continued)

clauses that preserved Israel's prerogative to conduct operations in those areas for purposes of its own security.

[108] For further information on UNRWA, see CRS Report RS22967, *U.S. Foreign Aid to the Palestinians*, by Jim Zanotti; and CRS Report RS21668, *United Nations Relief and Works Agency for Palestine Refugees in the Near East (UNRWA)*, by Rhoda Margesson.

[109] See FY2011 Congressional Budget Justification for Foreign Operations, Department of State (Volume 2), p. 86, available at http://www.state.gov/documents/organization/137936.pdf: "U.S. government support for UNRWA directly contributes to the U.S. strategic interest of meeting the humanitarian needs of Palestinians, while promoting their self-sufficiency. UNRWA plays a stabilizing role in the Middle East through its assistance programs, serving as an important counterweight to extremist elements."

[110] See Dunne, op. cit.

- Whether to grant the U.S. President discretion—under certain conditions and/or for specific purposes—to waive aid restrictions relating to a power-sharing government that includes Hamas and does not meet the Section 620K principles.

Secretary of State Hillary Rodham Clinton gave testimony at an April 2009 congressional hearing regarding the possibility of Hamas members serving in a PA government that would accept the Quartet principles and/or the Section 620K principles. She stated that "we are currently funding the Lebanese government, which has Hezbollah in it" because of a U.S. interest in supporting a government working to prevent the "further incursion of extremism."[111]

U.S. Assistance to Israel to Counter Rocket Threat

The Obama Administration and both houses of Congress have proposed funding to support Israel's development of a short-range missile defense system known as Iron Dome that is designed to counter the rocket threat from Hamas. The United States and Israel also are co-developing a missile defense system known as David's Sling that could potentially be deployed against Hamas's longer-range rockets.[112] For fuller detail on this subject, see CRS Report RL33222, *U.S. Foreign Aid to Israel*, by Jeremy M. Sharp; and CRS Report RL33476, *Israel: Background and Relations with the United States*, by Carol Migdalovitz.

Countering Financial and Smuggling Networks

Terrorist Designations and Legal Action

As discussed elsewhere in this report (see "Charities and Individuals" and **Appendix A**), U.S. executive orders and designations dating from 1995 that identify Hamas, affiliated organizations, and some of its leaders as terrorists (see **Table 4**) have authorized efforts, including those in concert with other international actors, to target Hamas funding sources. As also discussed elsewhere, existing anti-terrorism legislation has been used by U.S. courts to find U.S. citizens and/or organizations civilly and criminally liable for their material support of Hamas. Congress could evaluate how it might

- support the Administration's anti-terrorism financial and legal actions;
- mandate or advocate complementary or alternative actions; and
- provide greater oversight.

Some analysts believe that the effectiveness of U.S. cooperation with Israel, the PA, and other international actors in freezing Hamas's assets and global financial transfers has hindered Hamas's capacity to carry out terrorist attacks and significantly influenced its political decisions over the past decade—including its attempt to seek popular legitimacy in 2005-2006 Palestinian elections and its allegedly increased reliance on Iranian support.[113] Even though Hamas

---

[111] Transcript of House Appropriations Subcommittee on State, Foreign Operations and Related Programs hearing: "Supplemental Request," April 23, 2009.

[112] U.S.-Israel cooperation also takes place on a missile defense system known as "Arrow" that targets rockets of a longer range that what Hamas may currently possess.

[113] See, e.g., Milton-Edwards and Farrell, op. cit.

physically controls Gaza, the legal banking system there remains answerable to the PA in the West Bank and still applies controls in deference to U.S. policy.[114] Most analysts believe, therefore, that smuggling cash and valuable goods (trade-based money laundering) through the Gaza-Sinai tunnels remains a preferred option for Hamas.[115] Increasing scrutiny of charities and perhaps the specter of legal liability have reduced the effectiveness of Hamas financing networks in North America and Europe. Yet, political sensitivity to Hamas's popularity among Arab populations and an inclination to hedge bets on the outcome of the Fatah-Hamas rivalry may make Arab governments less likely to crack down on their own charities, even under U.S. pressure.

Sanctions on Iran and Syria

U.S. and international sanctions against Iran and Syria appear not to have had a significant effect on the two regimes' support for Hamas.[116] However, supporters of the sanctions may believe that even if the sanctions do not compel Iran and Syria to curtail or cease support for Hamas, they might make the two regimes' future support for Hamas less robust and effective. If sanctions weaken Iran and Syria in general terms, one could argue, resources and efforts allocated to helping Hamas and other potential proxies could be redirected to core internal matters related to regime survival. One, however, also might argue the reverse—that weaker Iranian and Syrian regimes could be *more* rather than *less* likely to sponsor potential proxies in order to draw domestic attention away from internal problems and focus it on common external adversaries and issues of regional or international concern.

Anti-Smuggling Efforts in Egypt and Elsewhere

The ongoing Israeli-Egyptian closure regime—consisting of an Israeli naval blockade plus heavy restrictions on the passage of people and goods through land crossings—places most of the focus of other anti-smuggling efforts on the Gaza-Sinai tunnels. Targeting these tunnels, however, remains problematic. The State Department's Country Reports on Terrorism 2009 said that "Israeli officials asserted that Egypt took steps to prevent arms smuggling from the Sinai into Gaza, but can do much more in terms of arresting, prosecuting, and incarcerating smugglers, destroying tunnel infrastructure, and providing socio-economic alternatives for Bedouin involved in smuggling activities."[117]

Egypt, with U.S. support, is nearing completion of an underground fence at its border with Gaza:

> United States army engineers are helping Egypt build the 6-8 km long steel wall, which is scheduled for completion in 2011. It was designed in the US and reportedly fits together like a jigsaw. The border is approximately 14 km long in total, but it is impossible to tunnel under the 5 km stretch approaching the sea, meaning that the wall is designed to cover all potential areas of tunnel construction. It has been bomb proofed and the 40 cm thick steel is

---

[114] Sayigh, *"We serve the people"…*, op. cit.

[115] See, e.g., Omar Karmi, "Going underground – Egypt's new wall may destabilize Gaza," *Jane's Intelligence Review*, March 12, 2010.

[116] For general information on sanctions against Iran and Syria, see CRS Report RS20871, *Iran Sanctions*, by Kenneth Katzman; and CRS Report RL33487, *Syria: Background and U.S. Relations*, by Jeremy M. Sharp.

[117] U.S. State Department, "Country Reports on Terrorism 2009," Chapter 2. Country Reports: Middle East and North Africa Overview, available at http://www.state.gov/s/ct/rls/crt/2009/140886.htm.

super-strength, although these factors, if Abu Murrad [a Qassam Brigades commander] is to be believed, have not proved impervious. The wall is designed to run as deep as 25 m, representing a major construction project.[118]

Many observers, however, remain skeptical because of the ineffectiveness of past anti-smuggling efforts. According to some, smugglers have already penetrated the Egyptian underground border fence and Hamas remains able to count on tunnels for money and weapons.[119] Egypt's inability or unwillingness to fully shut down tunnel traffic shows that external influence on its actions may have distinct limits. Egypt's motivations with regard to the Gaza-Sinai border are unique and complex—influenced by factors such as Hamas's potential to fan Islamist sentiment in Egyptian politics, fear that Israel might seek to transfer responsibility for Gaza to Egypt, Egypt's historical relationship to Gaza, a desire to accommodate traditional economic and cultural practices in Sinai, and comfort with the status quo.[120]

For additional information on U.S. support for Egyptian anti-smuggling measures, see CRS Report RL33003, *Egypt: Background and U.S. Relations*, by Jeremy M. Sharp; and CRS Report RL34346, *The Egypt-Gaza Border and its Effect on Israeli-Egyptian Relations*, by Jeremy M. Sharp.

Some analysts argue that easing or ending the Israeli-Egyptian closure regime, and hence facilitating normalized trade in everyday goods, would facilitate a narrower and potentially more effective military, intelligence, and law enforcement focus on keeping money and weapons out.[121] Although restrictions on non-dual-use goods entering Gaza from Israel were loosened in June 2010, the continued Israeli restriction on exports largely limits the goods legally entering Gaza to those provided through humanitarian aid.

Near the end of Operation Cast Lead in January 2009, the Bush Administration signed a memorandum of understanding with the Israeli government pledging additional U.S. support to counter weapons smuggling through a "multi-dimensional, results-oriented effort with a regional focus and international components working in parallel," including efforts to counter societal incentives for smuggling.[122] In March 2009, eight NATO member states agreed with the United States on a Gaza anti-smuggling program that "provides a comprehensive platform for enhanced cooperation and coordination in the areas of information and intelligence sharing; diplomatic engagement; and military and law enforcement activities."[123] Actions ascribed by most reports to Israel have occasionally occurred, including the January 2009 bombing of an apparent arms-smuggling convoy in Sudan moving in the direction of the Egypt-Gaza border[124] and the February

---

[118] Karmi, op. cit.

[119] See Ben Knight, "New Israeli-Egyptian border barrier has more than one purpose," *Deutsche Welle*, November 14, 2010. This article claimed that a new Israeli project to build a fence along the Israel-Egypt border might also target the Gaza-Egypt smuggling tunnels, although Egyptian officials have denied this. Ibid.

[120] See Karmi, op. cit.

[121] Colloquium attended by CRS at major U.S. think tank, October 2010.

[122] "Text of U.S.-Israel Agreement to End Gaza Arms Smuggling," *Ha'aretz*, January 17, 2009. Shortly afterward, the United States interdicted the Cypriot-flagged ship *Monchegorsk* in the Red Sea after it reportedly left Iran with weapons-related equipment.

[123] U.S. Department of State, "U.S. Welcomes Agreement on Gaza Weapons Smuggling," March 16, 2009, available at http://www.state.gov/r/pa/prs/ps/2009/03/120436.htm. The eight NATO member-states are Canada, Denmark, France, Germany, Italy, the Netherlands, Norway, and the United Kingdom.

[124] "How Israel Foiled an Arms Convoy Bound for Hamas," *Time*, March 30, 2009.

2010 assassination of Qassam Brigades leader Mahmoud al Mahbouh during his trip to allegedly purchase weapons from Iranian sources in Dubai.[125] It is not known whether those or similar actions involved intelligence sharing.

Countering Hamas Media

In March 2010, the Treasury Department named Hamas's Al Aqsa Television as a specially designated global terrorist (SDGT), thus allowing the United States to target Al Aqsa's finances. Three months later, in June 2010, France's official broadcast regulator ordered the French satellite operator Eutelsat to cease broadcast of Al Aqsa (which was carried through one of its satellites by Bahrain-based Noorsat).[126] This occurred following repeated urgings from the European Commission that Al Aqsa's programming violated European anti-incitement laws. It is unclear whether the U.S. designation of Al Aqsa also might have influenced the regulator's decision.

The 111th Congress considered legislation to counter Hamas incitement. H.R. 2278, which passed the House of Representatives on December 8, 2009 (by a vote of 395-3), and was referred to the Senate Foreign Relations Committee, would seek to make it U.S. policy to urge all parties with influence over satellite transmissions to halt broadcasts of Hamas-run Al Aqsa TV and similar channels (including Hezbollah's Al Manar TV) and to consider implementing punitive measures against satellite providers that do not halt such broadcasts. H.R. 2278 also would require an annual presidential report to Congress on "anti-American incitement to violence" that would include a country-by-country breakdown of (1) all media outlets that engage in such incitement and (2) all satellite providers that carry programming classified as such incitement.[127]

Addressing Hamas in a Regional Context

Another possible way to approach Hamas is by seeking to persuade other regional actors to cease support for Hamas or to influence Hamas to act more in accordance with U.S. interests. Although the United States and much of the Western world regards Hamas as a terrorist organization, it is regarded differently in many Middle Eastern states. As discussed above, Hamas is actively supported by Iran and Syria. Most others, including not only Qatar and Turkey, but also those considered to be the United States' closest Arab allies (such as Egypt, Jordan, and Saudi Arabia) acknowledge that Hamas is an integral part of Palestinian society and needs to be involved in both an internal Palestinian political solution and an Israeli-Palestinian peace. They maintain

---

[125] The Mahbouh killing, ascribed by most reports to the Israeli Mossad, caused a diplomatic backlash against Israel because the purported assassins used falsified or fraudulently obtained European and Australian passports to gain entry to Dubai. For a detailed account, see Alon Ben-David, "Spy games – Mossad returns to form," *Jane's Intelligence Review*, June 23, 2010.

[126] An Israeli organization has reported, however, that Hamas later agreed to a new Al Aqsa broadcast deal with Kuwait-based Gulfsat, which also broadcasts using a Eutelsat satellite. Intelligence and Terrorism Information Center, "Hamas' Al-Aqsa TV has circumvented the French media regulator's ban," July 12, 2010, available at http://www.terrorism-info.org.il/malam_multimedia/English/eng_n/html/hamas_e120.htm. Al Aqsa is also broadcast through Arab League-owned, Saudi Arabia-based Arabsat.

[127] It is unclear whether the executive branch would consider such legislation binding on its formulation of U.S. policy. On September 9, 2008 (during the 110th Congress), the House of Representatives passed H.Res. 1069 (by a 409-1 vote), which condemned Hamas's Al Aqsa TV (among other Middle East TV channels, including Al Manar) for anti-Israel, anti-Semitic, and anti-U.S. incitement and called upon satellite TV providers Arabsat (Arab League-owned, Saudi-based) and Eutelsat (privately owned, France-based) to cease transmitting Al Aqsa programming.

---

contact with Hamas to varying degrees and are sensitive to the strong support for Hamas believed to exist among their populations.

Oversight

Inclusion of Hamas in Negotiations?[128]

A major open question regarding congressional oversight of Administration policy is whether Hamas, with which U.S. government representatives are currently prohibited from having contact, could be included (either directly or indirectly) in U.S.-facilitated final-status negotiations between Israel and the Palestinians—in the event it wanted to be included. Acquiescing to the inclusion of Hamas in the peace process in some manner could involve its integration or reintegration into existing Palestinian leadership structures such as the PA and the PLO.

The Obama Administration has not departed from the Bush Administration's stance on Hamas. It has conditioned Hamas's participation in the peace process on its meeting the Quartet principles. The U.S. Special Envoy for Middle East Peace, former Senator George Mitchell, routinely cites distinguishing factors between the inclusion of the Irish Republican Army-affiliated Sinn Fein in the talks he brokered over Northern Ireland in the 1990s and the exclusion of Hamas in Israeli-Palestinian negotiations—the main one being Hamas's unwillingness to renounce violence as a means to redress its grievances. A number of meetings by former U.S. officials with senior Hamas leaders since 2009, however, has led some to wonder if the Administration might be open to indirect or secret talks with Hamas even in the absence of its acceptance of the Quartet principles.[129] In an October 2010 *Newsweek* interview, Khaled Meshaal said that one day U.S. officials "will not have any other alternative except to hear from Hamas and listen to Hamas."[130]

Any possibility of U.S. policy shifts regarding Hamas's role, however, could trigger heated debate. Those opposing policy shifts say dealing with Hamas would likely strengthen its political hand at the expense of Abbas and other more moderate Palestinians, allowing the movement to argue that its hardline tactics with Israel are more effective than Abbas's approach. They also might say that any move toward legitimizing Hamas and integrating it into Palestinian organs of governance such as the PLO or the PA could embolden it and other Palestinian militants to use these organs of governance to mount attacks on Israel—either before or after the establishment of a Palestinian state.[131] Those favoring policy shifts might say that Hamas is less likely to attack

---

[128] For more on this subject, see "The Role of Hamas" in CRS Report R40092, *Israel and the Palestinians: Prospects for a Two-State Solution*, by Jim Zanotti.

[129] Charles Levinson, "U.S. Ex-Officials Engage with Hamas," *Wall Street Journal*, April 2, 2010. Several former U.S. officials signed the 2009 U.S./Middle East Project report submitted to the Obama Administration that advocated taking a more "pragmatic approach" toward Hamas. The report acknowledged that direct U.S. engagement with Hamas might not now be practical, but recommended that the United States "offer [Hamas] inducements that will enable its more moderate elements to prevail, and cease discouraging third parties from engaging with Hamas in ways that might help clarify the movement's views and test its behavior." Zbigniew Brzezinksi, Chuck Hagel, et al., "A Last Chance for a Two-State Israel-Palestine Agreement: A Bipartisan Statement on U.S. Middle East Peacemaking," 2009 U.S./Middle East Project, available at http://www.usmep.us/bipartisan_recommendations/A_Last_Chance_for_a_Two-State_Israel-Palestine_Agreement.pdf.

[130] Babak Dehghanpisheh and Ranya Kadri, "Hamas Sticks to the Hard Line," *Newsweek*, October 14, 2010.

[131] These opponents might assert that Hamas should be dealt with only after it is marginalized. Israel did not agree to formal negotiations with Yasser Arafat of the PLO or with other historical Arab adversaries of Israel—such as former (continued...)

Israel if it is made a stakeholder that is accountable to revived Palestinian hopes of a Palestinian state.[132]

The U.S. military perceives the ongoing Israeli-Palestinian conflict as a growing threat to other U.S. interests in the region. In testimony before the Senate Armed Services Committee in March 2010, then U.S. Central Command (CENTCOM) commander (and current commander of the International Security Assistance Force in Afghanistan) General David Petraeus stated:

> The enduring hostilities between Israel and some of its neighbors present distinct challenges to our ability to advance our interests in the AOR [CENTCOM's area of responsibility]. Israeli-Palestinian tensions often flare into violence and large-scale armed confrontations. The conflict foments anti-American sentiment, due to a perception of U.S. favoritism for Israel. Arab anger over the Palestinian question limits the strength and depth of U.S. partnerships with governments and peoples in the AOR and weakens the legitimacy of moderate regimes in the Arab world. Meanwhile, al-Qaeda and other militant groups exploit that anger to mobilize support. The conflict also gives Iran influence in the Arab world through its clients, Lebanese Hizballah and Hamas.[133]

If the military's perception of Israeli-Palestinian tensions as a challenge to its objectives holds or expands, pressure could build for greater efforts to counteract these tensions. Such pressure may in turn lead to more urgent discussion of alternatives to prevent the expansion of Hamas's influence.[134] Some analysts who remain skeptical of Hamas's ultimate capacity for moderation nevertheless believe that the United States could gain some marginal or temporary advantages through some form of direct or indirect engagement of Hamas leaders (or some of them). Such efforts could be part of either a broad "carrots and sticks" strategy or a narrower focus on issues such as improving the economic and humanitarian situation in Gaza.[135] This is partly because these analysts do not see better alternatives for addressing the reality of Hamas and the leverage it holds. They sometimes cite U.S. willingness to engage or to consider engaging Sunni insurgents in Iraq and Taliban elements in Afghanistan as possible precedents.[136] Some high-ranking former

---

(...continued)

Egyptian President Anwar Sadat and King Hussein of Jordan—until it had established a position of strength relative to each of them. Some might say that doing this helped lead to diplomatic breakthroughs in each case. However, at a February 2009 hearing of the House Foreign Affairs Subcommittee on the Middle East and South Asia, Carnegie Endowment for International Peace analyst Michele Dunne provided an explanation for why the analogy may not apply to Hamas: "Regarding Hamas, I think that our problem as the United States is we want Hamas to walk the road that the PLO walked 20 years ago. And Hamas sees very well that the PLO walked that road, and it failed." See Transcript of Hearing, "Gaza After the War: What Can Be Built on the Wreckage," House Foreign Affairs Subcommittee on the Middle East and South Asia, February 12, 2009, available at http://foreignaffairs.house.gov/111/47420.pdf.

[132] See Joshua Mitnick, "As Peace Talks Sputter, Israelis and Palestinians Eye Plan B," *Christian Science Monitor*, September 15, 2008.

[133] Prepared statement of General David Petraeus, Senate Armed Services Committee Hearing, March 16, 2010, available at http://armed-services.senate.gov/statemnt/2010/03%20March/Petraeus%2003-16-10.pdf.

[134] See Mark Perry, "Red Team," *foreignpolicy.com*, June 30, 2010; Bilal Y. Saab, "What Do Red Teams Really Do?", *foreignpolicy.com*, September 3, 2010.

[135] See, e.g., Byman, op. cit.; Cambanis, "Letter from Gaza," op. cit.; Peter Beinart, "Hamas: U.S. Diplomacy's Final Frontier," *Time*, May 1, 2009; Muriel Asseburg, "Ending the Gaza Blockade – But How?", German Institute for International and Security Affairs (SWP), July 2010, available at http://www.swp-berlin.org/common/get_document.php?asset_id=7274.

[136] Beinart, op. cit.

Israeli officials, such as Ephraim Halevy (former Mossad director) and Giora Eiland (former head of Israel's National Security Council) also have advocated negotiating with Hamas.[137]

International Dimensions

Future debates might take place over whether the United States should actively dissuade others in the international community—particularly European actors—from engagement with and contributions to Hamas.[138] Although the other Quartet members formally espouse the Quartet principles, Russia has regular dealings with Hamas, legislators from various EU countries have met publicly with Khaled Meshaal and other Hamas leaders, and Hamas representatives claim that high-ranking European officials—including ambassadors—are talking to them regularly.[139] Some analysts believe that Khaled Meshaal's media overtures following President Obama's 2009 Cairo speech were largely aimed at gaining EU (if not U.S.) acceptance of a Hamas role in Palestinian affairs and/or the peace process without having to commit to the Quartet principles. Some might argue that European governments could be useful as go-betweens for Hamas and the United States, while others might counter that the go-between role may have limited utility— using Bush Administration-era European diplomacy with Iran as a case in point.

Activism and discourse on the international stage present additional challenges for U.S. policy regarding Hamas. The *Mavi Marmara* Gaza flotilla incident in May 2010 drew international attention—encouraged by Turkey—to the Gaza closure regime, leading the Obama Administration to persuade Israel to loosen restrictions on the importation of non-dual-use items such as food and medical supplies, and to greater relaxations by Egypt of the Rafah border crossing. This highlighted that even though the United States might be wary of pressing hard to change the status quo in Gaza, lest Hamas is boosted as a result, outside actors and events could in some cases force a response. Additional attempts to break the naval blockade are expected. For further details, see CRS Report R41275, *Israel's Blockade of Gaza, the Mavi Marmara Incident, and Its Aftermath*, by Carol Migdalovitz. The example established by the Turkey-based Islamist non-governmental organization IHH (Foundation for Human Rights and Freedoms and Humanitarian Relief), the lead sponsor of the flotilla, could inspire organizations that sympathize with Hamas, but seek to avoid sanctions for materially supporting it, to find creative ways to provide moral and political support.

Additionally, international investigations of both the May 2010 flotilla incident and Operation Cast Lead, as well as the publicity surrounding these investigations, have demonstrated that the United States has limited capacity to influence the direction of the debate. Attempts by the United States, Israel, and several European states to draw attention to Hamas's alleged culpability for recklessly endangering civilians during Operation Cast Lead, unjust and inhumane treatment of political opponents, and the difficult conditions faced by Gaza's population have generally been

---

[137] Byman, op. cit.

[138] On the previous occasions in which Hamas participated in the PA government from 2006-2007, the European Union joined the United States in refusing to provide direct assistance to the PA. There are indications, however, that Europeans might be less willing to follow the U.S. lead in the event that another PA government including Hamas is formed. See Muriel Asseburg and Paul Salem, "No Euro-Mediterranean Community without peace," EU Institute for Security Studies and European Institute of the Mediterranean, September 2009, available at http://www.iss.europa.eu/uploads/media/10Papers-01.pdf.

[139] Andrew Rettman, "EU Countries Practice 'Secret' Diplomacy, Hamas Says," *euobserver.com*, September 14, 2009.

countered by representatives of other governments at various U.N. bodies who focus their criticism on Israel for alleged violations of international law.

For example, the *Report of the U.N. Fact Finding Mission on the Gaza Conflict* (commonly known as the "Goldstone Report," after South African judge Richard Goldstone, the mission's leader), which was endorsed by the U.N. Human Rights Council and the U.N. General Assembly in the fall of 2009, has generated controversy because of what many U.S. officials and analysts have deemed its disproportionate and hyperbolic condemnation of Israeli strategy and actions during the conflict.[140] Most critics of the report believe that it did not sufficiently investigate or criticize Hamas for endangering Gaza's civilian population (including its allegedly intentional use of hospitals, schools, mosques, and residential neighborhoods as command and operations centers or as weapons caches, and of its civilians as "human shields"[141]). On November 3, 2009, the House of Representatives passed H.Res. 867 ("Calling on the President and the Secretary of State to oppose unequivocally any endorsement or further consideration of the 'Report of the United Nations Fact Finding Mission on the Gaza Conflict' in multilateral fora") by a vote of 344-36 (with 22 voting "present").

Conclusion

Hamas's integral role in Palestinian society and politics is seen by many as problematic because it is devoted to violent opposition to Israel. U.S. efforts to deter, transform, marginalize, or neutralize Hamas have at most achieved temporary or partial success. It is possible to conclude that U.S. and other international support for Israel and the PA/PLO/Fatah has been counterproductive to some extent when comparing Hamas's domestic, regional, and international strength in the early 1990s—measured by factors such as popularity, military force, and leverage with other actors (including Israel and Fatah)—to its current strength. Hamas routinely portrays U.S. efforts to counter its influence as part of an agenda to weaken Palestinians at the expense of Israel, hoping to convince Palestinians of Israel's implacability and of the futility of peace negotiations aimed at Palestinian statehood. Factional and geographical divisions—reflected in Hamas's control of Gaza and the Abbas-led PA's control of the West Bank—present fundamental dilemmas both for prospects for a two-state solution and for the future of Palestinian democracy.

U.S. policy and law reject dealings with and aid to Hamas or any PA government that includes Hamas without the acceptance of conditions that appear antithetical to Hamas's core principles. This could limit the Administration's ability to offer incentives even if regional conditions present possible advantages to doing so for U.S., Israeli, and/or Palestinian interests.

The Israeli-Egyptian closure regime in Gaza and various U.S. and international initiatives constrain and isolate Hamas to a point and may exacerbate internal organizational tensions and tactical disagreements. Overall, however, Hamas maintains a unified public stance on its core principle of violent opposition to Israel. It continues to threaten Israel through its rockets and the

---

[140] The Goldstone Report, dated September 25, 2009, is available at http://www2.ohchr.org/english/bodies/hrcouncil/specialsession/9/FactFindingMission.htm.

[141] The Goldstone Report found that Israel used Palestinian civilians as human shields during Operation Cast Lead, while stating that Israel had not provided sufficient evidence for a finding that Hamas had done the same. Ibid. In October 2010, an Israeli military court convicted two IDF soldiers of reckless endangerment and conduct unbecoming for using a nine-year-old Gaza boy to check suspected booby-traps. "Two Israeli soldiers guilty of using human shield in Gaza," *BBC News*, October 3, 2010, available at http://www.bbc.co.uk/news/world-middle-east-11462635.

possibility of other attacks and to receive assistance from Iran, Syria, Hezbollah, and private individuals and organizations. Additionally, Gaza's poor humanitarian conditions and morale contribute to an image of Hamas-as-victim and to local and international hostility toward Israel. In this context, any U.S. policy decision going forward will likely present considerable risks and difficult trade-offs.

Appendix A. Historical Background and U.S. Policy

Pre-1987: Hamas's Emergence

Hamas's politicization and militarization can be traced to the first Palestinian intifada ("uprising") that began in the Gaza Strip in 1987 in resistance to the Israeli occupation. Its precursor, Al Mujamma al Islami (known simply as Mujamma, or "The Islamic Center"), was established in Israeli-occupied Gaza in the 1970s under the auspices of the Palestinian Muslim Brotherhood, which had links to Muslim Brotherhood chapters in Egypt and Jordan and later developed links to branches elsewhere—most notably among Palestinian refugees and expatriates living in Kuwait. Sheikh Ahmed Yassin, the group's leader, concentrated the Mujamma's activities on religious and social services, following some models provided by the Egyptian and Jordanian Muslim Brotherhood branches, whose open political activism was repressed by state authorities. Yassin's and his associates' activities—which led to Hamas's founding—were countenanced and sometimes supported by Israel, which believed the Islamists to be a convenient foil for the secular nationalist factions such as Fatah that Israel then perceived to be greater threats.[142]

Motivation to become more politically active grew within Mujamma and the Palestinian Muslim Brotherhood after the 1979 Iranian Revolution led many in the Middle East to imagine the possibilities of political Islam, and in light of increased Palestinian concern for the status of the West Bank, Gaza, and Palestinian refugees following the deferral of the Palestinian question by the Israel-Egypt peace treaty of 1979 and Israel's 1982 invasion of Lebanon that forced the Palestine Liberation Organization (PLO) into exile in Tunisia. The formation in Gaza of other armed resistance groups such as Palestinian Islamic Jihad (PIJ) created pressure for the Palestinian Brotherhood to arm. Yassin's efforts to help the organization stockpile weapons led to his arrest by Israel in 1984, but the Brotherhood's gradual transformation into a militant organization regained momentum following Yassin's release in a 1985 prisoner swap. Yassin and his associates, who proceeded with outside support from their colleagues in Kuwait and elsewhere, officially established Hamas in 1987 when the first Palestinian intifada (or uprising) provided widespread Palestinian support for resistance against Israel.

1987-1995: Gaining Attention

In Hamas's early years during the first intifada, international political attention remained focused on Yasser Arafat's Fatah movement and the PLO, under the rationale that other Palestinian groups had marginal political legitimacy or would take cues from Arafat. When Israel deported several top Hamas leaders to southern Lebanon in December 1992 (along with several other Palestinian Islamists—more than 400 total) in response to a number of Hamas kidnappings and killings of Israeli soldiers, the United States joined human rights organizations in pressuring Israel to repatriate the leaders to the West Bank and Gaza, which it did in late 1993.[143]

---

[142] Andrew Higgins, "How Israel Helped to Spawn Hamas," *Wall Street Journal*, January 25, 2009.

[143] Some believe this Israeli measure strengthened, rather than weakened, Hamas. Not only did its deported leaders persevere and bond through the hardships of a year in exile, but they also cultivated relations with and received mentorship from the Iran-backed Hezbollah movement before being repatriated to the West Bank and Gaza in 1993 as a result of pressure on Israel from human rights organizations and the United States. See Paul McGeough, *Kill Khalid: The Failed Mossad Assassination and the Rise of Hamas*, The New Press, New York, 2009, p. 68.

Following the signing of the Israel-PLO Declaration of Principles (or Oslo Accord) in September 1993, Hamas joined with other Islamist and some leftist Palestinian factions in rejecting Oslo framework limiting Palestinian national aspirations to the West Bank and Gaza (and thus giving up the national dream for all of "Palestine" as it existed under the British Mandate) and creating multi-tiered zones of Palestinian self-rule circumscribed by a continuing Israeli occupation whose future remained subject to negotiation. Hamas also refused to participate in elections for the new Palestinian Authority (until subsequent developments led to a change of strategy in 2005-2006).

Hamas and other rejectionist groups engaged in sporadic attacks on Israeli targets inside the Palestinian territories. However, following a February 1994 shooting and grenade attack by an Israeli settler that killed 29 and injured several more Palestinians worshiping at the historic Mosque of Abraham in the West Bank city of Hebron, Hamas significantly shifted its strategy. It began a spate of attacks aimed at civilians in Israel, including its first use of suicide bombings in crowded public places.

Meanwhile U.S. Federal Bureau of Investigation investigations, Israeli investigations, and media reporting revealed that Hamas had apparently been recruiting and fundraising on U.S. soil since its inception. As mentioned in the main body of the report (see "Charities and Individuals"), an alleged hub of Hamas financing was the Holy Land Foundation for Relief and Development headquartered near Dallas, TX, and which had offices in California, New Jersey, and Illinois. As this information became public and Hamas and other Palestinian groups continued attacks on Israeli targets (sometimes killing or injuring U.S. citizens), pressure mounted for the Clinton Administration to act.

1995-2004: Violence and International Opposition

In January 1995, then President Bill Clinton signed Executive Order 12947, which blocked the assets of and prohibited U.S. transactions with Hamas and 11 other specially designated terrorist organizations (SDTs) deemed threats to the Middle East peace process, including the Israeli extremist groups Kach and Kahane Chai.[144]

Meanwhile, Israel was vigorously pursuing operatives from Hamas and pressuring the newly formed Palestinian Authority (PA) led by Yasser Arafat to crack down as well. Israel had allowed the PA to establish internal security forces in Gaza and the West Bank from former PLO and Fatah militias. Arafat encouraged the formation of additional paramilitary and intelligence organizations populated with many close Arafat associates that Israel tolerated (despite their not being sanctioned under the Oslo agreements) with the hope that they would help neutralize Hamas and other terrorist organizations. In addition to targeting Hamas militants, the PA forces periodically suppressed the activities of Hamas-affiliated charities and social organizations.

In early 1996, following another round of Hamas suicide bombings, the United States became actively involved in fostering Israeli-Palestinian security cooperation in combating terrorism. Likely determining that the paramilitary and intelligence organizations with personal ties to Arafat and patronage networks were more relevant than the official police, the Clinton Administration reportedly began providing these organizations with tens of millions of dollars in covert assistance through the Central Intelligence Agency (CIA), according to the *New York*

---

[144] Executive Order 12947 of January 23, 1995, "Prohibiting Transactions with Terrorists Who Threaten to Disrupt the Middle East Peace Process," available at http://www.treas.gov/offices/enforcement/ofac/legal/eo/12947.pdf.

Times.[145] The European Union also reportedly began a counterterrorism program.[146] Additionally, in October 1997, the State Department listed Hamas as a Foreign Terrorist Organization (FTO), shortly after a major September suicide bombing in a Jerusalem pedestrian shopping area that left one U.S. citizen among the dead and several others among the injured.

The fruits of U.S. counterterrorism assistance to the PA continue to be debated. Although Hamas suicide and other attacks did not immediately cease, they abated from the end of 1998 until the second Palestinian intifada (also known as the Al Aqsa intifada) began in September 2000. The effects of U.S. assistance are unclear partly because of its covert nature, and because of several other intervening factors—including Israeli counterterrorism actions and ongoing Israeli-Palestinian negotiations. Some observers point to the drop-off in attacks as evidence that U.S. assistance helped the PA prevent and deter terrorist attacks until the collapse of peace process negotiations in 2000. Others believe that although PA capacities were enhanced, Arafat's on-again, off-again crackdowns on Hamas and other militants were of little lasting value. Suspects detained to placate U.S. and Israeli pressure were often released shortly thereafter due to internal political pressure on Arafat and the PA not to appear to be "collaborating" with the Israelis or because of insufficient evidence owing to the political nature of the arrests.

Upon the outbreak of the second intifada in September 2000, Hamas demonstrated that it still had the capacity to carry out attacks inside Israel. Following Al Qaeda's attacks against multiple U.S. targets on September 11, 2001, then President George W. Bush issued Executive Order 13224 authorizing his Administration to take action domestically and in concert with international actors to suppress the activities and block the financing of a list of specially designated global terrorist individuals and organizations (SDGTs). Hamas was added to the list in October 2001, and the Holy Land Foundation for Relief and Development was added in December 2001. Six Hamas leaders (including Khaled Meshaal, Musa Abu Marzouk, and Osama Hamdan—see **Appendix C**), along with five Hamas-affiliated charities (four based in Europe, one based in Lebanon) were later added in August 2003.[147] Al Aqsa Television and Hamas's Islamic National Bank were added in March 2010.[148] As discussed in the main body of the report (see "Charities and Individuals"), a Hamas-related, Saudi Arabia-based organization known as the Union of Good was added to the list in November 2008.

Although some U.S. counterterrorism assistance to the Arafat-led PA continued during the second intifada, such assistance was complicated by the fact that offshoots (known as Tanzim and the Al Aqsa Martyrs' Brigades) from Arafat's own Fatah faction that included former PA security force commanders were participating in attacks on Israeli military and civilian targets—possibly with Arafat's tacit approval. Following the deadliest attack of the intifada in March 2002, a Hamas suicide bombing of the Park Hotel in Netanya during a Passover seder that killed 22 Israelis and injured over 100 more, Israel mounted Operation Defensive Shield. During March and April of 2002, the Israel Defense Forces (IDF) moved into major West Bank cities, established martial law, destroyed much of the PA's security and civilian infrastructure, and besieged Arafat's

---

[145] Elaine Sciolino, "Violence Thwarts C.I.A. Director's Unusual Diplomatic Role in Middle Eastern Peacemaking," *New York Times*, November 13, 2000. See also Vernon Loeb, "CIA Emerges to Resolve Mideast Disputes; Out of Shadows, Agency Is Directly Involved in Israeli-Palestinian Security Talks," *Washington Post*, September 30, 1998.

[146] See Brynjar Lia, *Building Arafat's Police*, Ithaca Press, Reading, UK, 2007, p. 300, et seq.

[147] U.S. Treasury Department, Office of Foreign Assets Control, "What You Need to Know About U.S. Sanctions," available at http://www.ustreas.gov/offices/enforcement/ofac/programs/terror/terror.pdf

[148] U.S. Treasury Department press release TG-594, "Treasury Designates Gaza-Based Business, Television Station for Hamas Ties," March 18, 2010, available at http://www.ustreas.gov/press/releases/tg594.htm.

compound in Ramallah. In the post-September 11 environment, the Bush Administration acquiesced to Israel's characterization of Operation Defensive Shield as a necessary counterterrorism operation. In June 2002, President Bush indicated that Arafat was no longer a trusted part of the peace process, and that future U.S. support for the PA would need to come through another leader.[149]

Hamas did not escape Israeli countermeasures. Israel embarked on a targeted assassination campaign, killing many top Hamas leaders in Gaza between 2002-2004, including co-founders Sheikh Ahmed Yassin and Abdel Aziz al Rantissi. As a natural consequence, the geographical locus of Hamas's leadership shifted to Khaled Meshaal and the political bureau in Damascus, where it is less vulnerable to Israeli assassination operations than in Gaza. Even though Hamas had to absorb the shock of losing much of its founding core, its reputation and institutions were strengthened relative to Fatah and the PA owing to the damage done to PA infrastructure and security institutions and to public confidence in Palestinian leadership. Additionally, Hamas was able to elevate its cause in the eyes of many Palestinians by portraying its assassinated leaders as lionized martyrs.

2005-2006: Israel's Gaza Disengagement and the Palestinian Legislative Council Election Campaign

During the second intifada, the popularity of Hamas began to increase as Fatah's fell. At the same time, the Israel Defense Forces (IDF) effectively dismantled the security organizations and infrastructure of the Fatah-dominated PA, which had the unintended consequence of leaving Fatah more vulnerable to domestic security threats. Cognizant of its increasing strength and popularity relative to Fatah, Hamas's leaders made the momentous decision in the spring of 2005 to participate in Palestinian Authority elections even as they maintained Hamas's rejection of the principle of Israeli-Palestinian agreement that had established the PA. Hamas made a strong showing in a series of municipal elections held in 2005. Still, many observers were surprised when Hamas won a controlling majority in the PLC in its first-ever national election campaign in January 2006, leading to its heightened international profile and current situation.

After Yasser Arafat's death in November 2004, the United States encouraged the emergence of a successor committed to the peace process. With the central figure of Palestinian nationalism gone, Hamas saw an opportunity. Mahmoud Abbas was elected to succeed Arafat as PA President in January 2005, an election that Hamas did not contest. Hamas had not participated in the initial Palestinian Legislative Council (PLC) elections of 1996 because of its opposition to the Oslo framework that created the PA and PLC. Yet, by late 2004, the situation was different. Hamas may have been feeling pressure to transform its international image from that of a militant group operating in the shadows to that of a political movement with domestic legitimacy. U.S. and international efforts to curb Hamas's activities and financing, combined with Israeli opposition, also may have played a part in Hamas's thinking, which one Palestinian analyst in Gaza explained as follows in 2006:

---

[149] The first attempt at cultivating an Arafat alternative under the rubric of the international Quartet's "Roadmap for Peace" effort in 2003 was to transfer several of Arafat's powers to Mahmoud Abbas as PA Prime Minister. Although an Arafat associate, Abbas had a reputation as an advocate for a negotiated peace with Israel, and was critical of the Palestinian turn to violence during the second intifada. The U.S. and international attempt to empower Abbas, however, proved abortive, as Arafat would not relinquish control over key PA security and financial power centers, and Abbas resigned in frustration in October 2003 after only six months in office.

> For two years now Hamas has been feeling that the jihadi approach was reaching a dead end…. It was classified as a terrorist movement by the US and some other countries. From this point it decided to log into the Palestinian political system. It felt besieged by the outside world. They froze all their money and stopped all its institutions. So they started seeking new legitimacy through the ballot box…. Not, I think, because they believe in democracy, but because they want legitimacy, to say to the world that they are a party or a movement that represents the Palestinian people through democratic elections.[150]

The 2006 PLC election (the first PLC election in 10 years) took place at a time when the Bush Administration was advocating for democratic elections throughout the Arab world, including in post-invasion Iraq, Lebanon, Egypt, and the Gulf. Abbas wanted to include Hamas in order to erase all doubt that Fatah remained the Palestinian people's clear choice to succeed Arafat, and Hamas agreed to participate as the "Change and Reform" party. The United States, the international community, and Israel acceded to this plan without preconditions for Hamas's involvement, partly because of the plan's popularity among Palestinians and the outside actors' desire to avoid interfering in internal Palestinian politics, and partly because the outside actors underestimated Hamas's prospects. Most pollsters and observers also underestimated Hamas's prospects, even if some had misgivings and forecast a close election.[151] Many analysts believe that Hamas received a boost from Israel's August 2005 disengagement from Gaza because it was amenable to the interpretation that Hamas precipitated it through resistance.[152]

The Bush Administration provided direct financial assistance to the PA to boost its public profile during the run-up to the elections, knowing that Palestinians closely identified the PA with Fatah given their overlapping leadership cadres. The U.S. Agency for International Development (USAID) allocated $2 million—purportedly at least double Hamas's entire campaign budget—for this media, public outreach, and public services initiative. It was coordinated by a U.S. contractor and Palestinian subcontractors through Abbas's office. According to the *Washington Post*, some involved in the project debated its wisdom, and the *Post* itself expressed concerns:

> The program highlights the central challenge facing the Bush administration as it promotes democracy in the Middle East. Free elections in the Arab world, where most countries have been run for years by unelected autocracies or unchallenged parties like Fatah, often result in strong showings by radical Islamic movements opposed to the policies of the United States and to its chief regional ally, Israel. But in attempting to manage the results, the administration risks undermining the democratic goals it is promoting.[153]

When elections took place in January 2006, Hamas only outpolled Fatah in the party-list vote 44% to 41%. Yet, Hamas deployed a superior campaign strategy that took advantage of division

---

[150] Interview with Ibrahim Ibrach, as quoted in Milton-Edwards and Farrell, op. cit., pp. 246-247.

[151] See Palestinian Center for Policy and Survey Research, Special Public Opinion Poll on the Upcoming Palestinian Elections (January 17-19, 2006), available at http://www.pcpsr.org/survey/polls/2006/preelectionsjan06.html (forecasting a 7% margin of victory for Fatah, with a 2% margin of error); Jerusalem Media and Communications Centre, Poll No. 56, January 2006, available at http://www.jmcc.org/documentsandmaps.aspx?id=444 (forecasting a 2% margin of victory for Fatah).

[152] A Hamas banner flown in Gaza shortly after the August 2005 disengagement read, in English, "Jerusalem and West Bank after Gaza HAMAS." Milton-Edwards and Farrell, op. cit., p. 246. See also Palestinian Center for Policy and Survey Research, Palestinian Public Opinion Poll #17 (September 7-9, 2005), available at http://www.pcpsr.org/survey/polls/2005/p17a.html: "On The Eve Of The Israeli Withdrawal From The Gaza Strip, 84% See It As Victory For Armed Resistance And 40% Give Hamas Most Of The Credit For It".

[153] Scott Wilson and Glenn Kessler, "U.S. Funds Enter Fray in Palestinian Elections," *Washington Post*, January 22, 2006.

---

and complacency among Fatah and its candidates to win individual geographical districts in greater proportion to Hamas's overall share of the vote and secure a majority of seats in the PLC. It is unclear whether U.S. involvement made a difference, but the perception that Hamas lunged ahead at campaign's end in the face of significant U.S. backing for its opponent fed claims that the U.S. strategy had backfired with the Palestinian public, negatively impacting views of U.S. competence in the region.[154]

2006-2010: Confronting an Empowered Hamas

Once Hamas's electoral victory was clear, Israel insisted that it would not cooperate with a PA that included a hostile Hamas, even discontinuing transfer of customs revenues it collected for the PA. The United States and other members of the international Quartet (European Union, Russia, United Nations) announced that Hamas would have to meet three conditions in order for a PA under its control to receive aid and political support: (1) recognize Israel's right to exist, (2) renounce violence, and (3) accept prior Israeli-Palestinian agreements.

Hamas and its incoming government ministers—led by Prime Minister Ismail Haniyeh—rejected the Quartet principles, and therefore began their term leading the PA government without access to U.S. and European aid. They turned to Gulf states, Iran, and Russia (despite Russia's status as a member of the Quartet), all of which were willing to provide funding under the rationale that Hamas had entered power legitimately through the established political process. The United States' and European Union's unwillingness to provide financial assistance to the elected government, on the heels of their support for the elections, was seen by many analysts as inconsistent with the principle of democracy both claimed to advocate for the region.[155]

Not wanting to contribute to possible destabilization of the West Bank and Gaza through an aid cutoff, Congress and the Bush Administration devised a way to bypass the Hamas-led PA ministries in delivering aid to Palestinians.[156] They continued humanitarian and development assistance through UNRWA and other international and non-governmental organizations that were subjected to increasing levels of U.S. government scrutiny to guard against enriching Hamas or its supporters.

Factional tensions worsened considerably following Fatah's defeat at the hands of Hamas. Although Abbas and Fatah formally accepted the PLC election results, Fatah loyalists with key roles in the PA civil service and security forces refused to accede to Hamas's control and actively sought to undermine it. The rivalry played out dramatically in Gaza, where Hamas was more strongly rooted than in the West Bank, and where the recent Israeli disengagement had left an uncertain security situation amid widespread political corruption and clan-dominated lawlessness.

---

[154] See, e.g., Glenn Kessler, "Bush Is Conciliatory in Accepting Victory of Hamas," *Washington Post*, January 27, 2006. In their 2010 book on Hamas, Beverley Milton-Edwards and Stephen Farrell wrote the following about the 2006 elections: "The foreign interventions proved pointless, even counterproductive. To neutralize them Hamas held back its closing message until the final days of the campaign—huge banners across the main streets of Palestinian cities which proclaimed: 'Israel and America say no to Hamas. What do you say?'" Milton-Edwards and Farrell, op. cit., p. 256.

[155] See, e.g., Rami G. Khouri, "On Democracy, Arabs Mistrust the American Messenger," *Daily Star* (Lebanon), February 4, 2006.

[156] The European Union also provided aid directly to Palestinians in the West Bank and Gaza for humanitarian and development purposes (including support for Gaza's power plant) through its Temporary International Mechanism (TIM).

Congress and the Administration addressed this situation by enacting the Palestinian Anti-Terrorism Act of 2006 (P.L. 109-446), which approved funding PA offices and security forces under the control of President Abbas, as contrasted with those controlled by Hamas-led government ministries. Lines of command and control over existing PA forces remained blurred, a legacy from Yasser Arafat's rule, so Fatah played on the loyalties of personnel to align most of the security forces with Abbas, and Hamas organized its own shadow "Executive Force" from its loyalists in Gaza. Instead of containing the situation, these developments appear to have escalated it.

Tensions did not abate significantly after the Mecca Accord of February 2007, a Saudi Arabia-brokered power-sharing deal that brought some Fatah members and independents into the Hamas-led government. This may have been the case in part because the United States and European Union did not believe the agreement changed the nature of the PA government sufficiently to justify the resumption of direct budgetary assistance to the PA.

The story of Hamas's takeover of the Gaza Strip and subsequent dismissal from power in the West Bank by Abbas in June 2007 is told in different ways from different perspectives. Some have cited U.S. deliberations with Abbas to support the idea that an offensive move against Hamas's government and security forces in Gaza was imminent.[157] Others say that Hamas was judiciously biding its time for the right moment to strike, but debate whether it intended to seize power in Gaza or simply weaken the PA forces targeting it.[158] Most can agree on certain basic facts. U.S., Canadian, and European training and consulting was provided to strengthen PA forces—headed by Fatah strongman Muhammad Dahlan—loyal to Abbas in Gaza. These forces, still systematically weakened from the second intifada, were less-than-optimally equipped, organized, and disciplined. When directly engaged by the Qassam Brigades and other Hamas-led forces, the PA forces loyal to Abbas gave way within a week, with many personnel fleeing to the West Bank or abstaining from the fight (including some who later chose to stay with the security forces after Hamas assumed their command). Hamas then seized the opportunity to secure full control over Gaza.[159]

The subsequent bifurcation of Palestinian leadership in the West Bank and Gaza resulted in U.S. and international support for the "caretaker" West Bank PA government led by Prime Minister Salam Fayyad that Abbas appointed, and even in renewed Israeli ties with the PA and PLO. Support for the PA remains a strategy the international community, with some exceptions, generally pursues in tandem with isolation of Hamas. Many Palestinians fear that the longer the West Bank and Gaza remain under divided leadership, the less likely restoration of unitary government over both territories will be, and the easier it could be for the societies to drift apart economically and culturally as well. As presidential, legislative, and even local elections continue to be postponed, some analysts warn of growing authoritarianism in both territories.[160]

Facing international isolation and the Israeli-Egyptian border closure regime, Hamas focused its energies on consolidating its control within Gaza. To preserve its status as an organization committed to resistance against an Israel that it cannot confront easily in a conventional warfare setting, Hamas has relied on smuggling rockets and mortars through the tunnels and firing them

---

[157] See David Rose, "The Gaza Bombshell," *Vanity Fair*, April 2008.

[158] See, e.g., Sayigh, *"We serve the people"...*, op. cit.

[159] A detailed account is found in Milton-Edwards and Farrell, op. cit., pp. 282-292.

[160] Nathan J. Brown, "Are Palestinians Building a State?", op. cit.

in concert with other militant groups. When these attacks led to Operation Cast Lead in 2008-2009, Hamas's forces were shown to be little match operationally for the IDF, but relatively few of its personnel were killed and the IDF did not attempt to eliminate its presence in Gaza or seize control of the territory. Hamas has portrayed its survival as victory, but many believe that Hamas did not expect the intensity of the Israeli operation and genuinely feared for the survival of its rule in Gaza, and, as a result, has since been more cautious about possible provocations.

U.S. humanitarian assistance to Gaza and comprehensive assistance to the West Bank continues, as does U.S. political support and assistance for anti-smuggling efforts on land and at sea. Under the various terrorist designations it has attached to Hamas, the United States collaborates with Israel and other governments to thwart Hamas financing and attack capabilities. Attempts at forwarding Israel-PLO peace negotiations are being facilitated by the United States, with Hamas conspicuously uninvited. Nevertheless, events such as the May 2010 *Mavi Marmara* flotilla incident and the reaction it provoked complicate U.S. policy towards Hamas because they demonstrate divisions in international approaches toward Gaza.

Appendix B. Key Dates in Hamas's History

Chronology

1946	Establishment of Palestinian Muslim Brotherhood
1948	Arab-Israeli war (Israeli war of independence/Palestinian nakba, or "catastrophe") leaves West Bank under Jordanian administration and Gaza Strip under Egyptian administration
1967	Six-Day Arab-Israeli war; Israel occupies West Bank (including East Jerusalem), Gaza Strip, Sinai Peninsula, and Golan Heights
1970-1971	Jordan evicts PLO through "Black September" military operations; PLO leadership relocates to Lebanon
1973	Yom Kippur War between Israel and Egypt
	Al Mujamma al Islami (the Islamic Center) established by Sheikh Ahmed Yassin and Muslim Brotherhood associates in Gaza Strip
1978	Muslim Brotherhood helps establish Islamic University in Gaza
1979	Israel-Egypt peace treaty; Palestinian question deferred
	Iranian Revolution
Early 1980s	Muslim Brotherhood branches in Gaza and West Bank develop ties with each other and with branches outside of the Palestinian territories—especially those with heavy representation from the Palestinian diaspora (such as in Kuwait)
1981	Palestinian Islamic Jihad established in Gaza Strip
1982	Israel invades Lebanon; PLO leadership forced to relocate to Tunisia
1984	Yassin imprisoned by Israel
1985	Yassin released in prisoner exchange
1987	Outbreak of first Palestinian intifada
	Establishment of Hamas as political and military resistance organization in Palestinian territories
1988	Hamas publishes its founding charter
1989	Yassin and several other Hamas leaders imprisoned by Israel in response to Hamas attacks on Israeli military targets (first of many waves of detentions and subsequent releases of Hamas leaders in Gaza and West Bank); Hamas outside leadership becomes more prominent
1990	Yassin sentenced to life in prison
1990-1991	Saddam Hussein's Iraq invades and occupies Kuwait and is expelled by a U.S.-led coalition in Operation Desert Storm; Hamas's outside leadership relocates from Kuwait to Jordan
1992-1993	Over 400 Hamas leaders and other Palestinian Islamists deported to southern Lebanon by Israel after the abduction and killing of an Israeli policeman; repatriated as a result of pressure from the United States and human rights organizations; consequently Hamas's leadership outside the Palestinian territories is elevated to a more important role within the movement
1993	Signing of Israel-PLO Declaration of Principles (Oslo Accord); Hamas and other Palestinian factions reject the agreement

1994	Israeli settler Baruch Goldstein kills 29 Palestinians at Mosque of Abraham in Hebron, West Bank
	Hamas retaliates with first suicide bombings in Israel; similar attacks will continue periodically before abating in 1997
	Establishment of Palestinian Authority with Yasser Arafat's arrival in Gaza
	Israel-Jordan peace treaty complicates Hamas's ongoing presence in Jordan
1995	United States designates Hamas and 11 other organizations obstructing the Middle East peace process as specially designated terrorists (SDTs)
	Musa Abu Marzouk, then Hamas politburo chief, arrested at New York's Kennedy Airport and remains in U.S. custody for nearly two years; Khaled Meshaal eventually succeeds him
	Assassination of Israeli prime minister Yitzhak Rabin by Israeli law student Yigal Amir
1996	Hamas kills 59 Israelis in Jerusalem, Tel Aviv, and Ashqelon in four suicide bombings (one in collaboration with Palestinian Islamic Jihad) within a two-week period in February and March
1997	Failed Israeli Mossad assassination attempt of Meshaal in Amman, Jordan following two Hamas street-side suicide bombings (21 killed) that summer in Jerusalem; Yassin released in exchange for release of Mossad agents in Jordanian custody
	State Department designates Hamas a Foreign Terrorist Organization (FTO)
1999	Hamas's politburo leaders imprisoned in Jordan and ultimately expelled to Doha, Qatar
2000	Failure to reach Israel-PLO final-status agreement at Camp David summit
	Second Palestinian intifada (Al Aqsa intifada) begins
2001	Hamas reinstitutes suicide bombings and other attacks on Israel; first rockets fired on Israeli targets from Gaza
	Hamas's politburo leaders relocate to Damascus, Syria, where Hamas's head shura council is located
	September 11 attacks in the United States by Al Qaeda
	United States designates Hamas a specially designated global terrorist (SDGT) in October (will add various Hamas leaders and affiliated organizations to SDGT in subsequent months and years)
2002	Hamas and Palestinian Islamic Jihad carry out suicide bombing at Park Hotel in Netanya during Passover seder, killing 30
2003	Council of the European Union adds Hamas to its consolidated list of terrorist organizations
2004	Hamas co-founders Yassin and Abdel Aziz al Rantissi are assassinated within less than a month of each other by Israeli airstrikes in Gaza
	Death of Yasser Arafat
2005	Hamas decides to participate in Palestinian elections; makes strong showing in municipal elections
	Israel withdraws its troops and settlers from Gaza Strip; resulting Palestinian rivalry for security primacy in Gaza begins

2006	Hamas wins majority in Palestinian Legislative Council election
	Hamas forms PA government under Prime Minister Ismail Haniyeh; United States and European Union cease aid to PA ministries, instead funneling aid through PA President Mahmoud Abbas or alternative mechanisms and organizations
	Palestinian militants abduct Israeli corporal Gilad Shalit near Gaza border and deliver him into Hamas's custody, helping spark limited conflict in Gaza Strip between Israel and Palestinian militants (including Hamas)
	Israel engages in conflict with Hezbollah in southern Lebanon (at the same time the conflict in Gaza continued) following Hezbollah's abduction and killing of Israeli soldiers near the Lebanese border
2007	Hamas and Fatah reach Mecca Accord for power-sharing PA government; United States and European Union refuse to resume aid to PA ministries
	After armed clash with PA/Fatah forces, Hamas gains control of Gaza Strip; Abbas dismisses Hamas ministers from PA government and appoints non-Hamas government headed by Prime Minister Salam Fayyad; PLC loses quorum to do business; Palestinian rocket attacks from Gaza on Israel and Israeli-Egyptian closure regime both intensify
	Israel declares Gaza a "hostile entity"
2008	Hamas breaks open Gaza-Egypt border crossing at Rafah; tens of thousands of Gazans pour into Egypt temporarily
	Hamas and Israel agree to informal cease-fire (brokered by Egypt)
	Cease-fire ends; Hamas resumes major rocket fire into Israel
2008-2009	Operation Cast Lead (Gaza conflict with Israel)
2009	Senator John Kerry and Representatives Brian Baird and Keith Ellison visit Gaza to assess humanitarian needs and to meet with U.N. officials (not Hamas officials); first congressional visits to Gaza since October 2003 roadside bombing of U.S. convoy by non-Hamas militants
	Goldstone Report released
	PA elections scheduled for president and for the Palestinian Legislative Council in January 2010 are canceled after Hamas announces it will not permit balloting in Gaza; PLO Central Council indefinitely extends terms of Mahmoud Abbas as PA President and of Palestinian Legislative Council
2010	Qassam Brigades operative Mahmoud al Mahbouh is murdered in a Dubai hotel room, an action ascribed by most reports to Israel
	MV Mavi Marmara flotilla incident and aftermath; Israel and Egypt ease Gaza closure regime (Israel allows greater importation of non-dual-use items)
	Coinciding with relaunch of direct Israel-PLO negotiations, Hamas militants stage two shooting attacks against Israeli settlers in the West Bank, killing four and injuring two

Appendix C. Major Hamas Leaders

Political Leaders

Outside of Gaza

Khaled Meshaal[161]

Khaled Meshaal, based in Damascus, is the chief of Hamas's politburo. He was named a specially designated global terrorist (SDGT) by the Treasury Department in August 2003.

Born in 1956 near Ramallah, Meshaal (alternate spellings: Mishal, Mashal) moved with his family to Jordan in 1967 following Israel's occupation of the West Bank in the Six-Day War. As a student and schoolteacher in Kuwait, he became a leader in the Palestinian Islamist movement. After the founding of Hamas in 1987, Meshaal led the Kuwaiti branch of the organization, then moved to Jordan in 1991 after Iraq's invasion of Kuwait. He took over as Hamas politburo chief following the 1995 U.S. arrest of then chief Musa Abu Marzouk.

In September 1997, Meshaal was targeted in Amman by the Mossad (Israel's foreign intelligence service) in an assassination attempt that became a major international incident—culminating in King Hussein of Jordan threatening to abrogate the 1994 Israel-Jordan peace treaty in order to get Binyamin Netanyahu (in his first stint as Israeli prime minister) to supply an antidote to the nerve toxin to which Meshaal had been exposed.[162] After the Hamas leadership was expelled from Jordan in November 1999, Meshaal first moved to Doha, Qatar, then settled two years later in Damascus, Syria. He became acknowledged as Hamas's overall leader in 2004, following the assassination of Abdel Aziz al Rantissi by Israel. Meshaal also serves as Hamas's top diplomat, traveling and meeting with various governments and political leaders (including his political rival Mahmoud Abbas, Iran, Turkey, Arab countries, Russia, European legislators, and former U.S. President Jimmy Carter).

Musa Abu Marzouk

Musa Abu Marzouk, born in 1951 in the Rafah refugee camp in Gaza, and now based in Damascus, is a deputy chief of Hamas's politburo. He was named an SDT in August 1995 and an SDGT in August 2003 by the Treasury Department.

Marzouk, a legal U.S. resident for 15 years during the 1980s and early 1990s, also played a key role in defining the relationship between Hamas's Gaza organization and its outside political leadership following the mass arrests of Hamas leaders in Gaza during the first intifada. Marzouk himself headed the outside leadership until 1995. He is credited as the mastermind behind the construction of Hamas's financial networks in the United States, including involvement with the Holy Land Foundation for Relief and Development. Marzouk was detained in New York's

---

[161] See also "Khaled Mishal, external leader, Hamas Political Bureau," *Jane's Intelligence Weekly*, December 16, 2009.

[162] For a detailed account of the failed assassination attempt and Meshaal's rise to power within Hamas, see McGeough, op. cit.

Kennedy Airport in July 1995 (after arriving on a flight from Jordan) following the naming of Hamas as an SDT in January 1995. Israel sought his extradition, but later dropped its request due to retaliation concerns and Marzouk rejoined Hamas's political bureau in Jordan in 1997, becoming deputy chief to Khaled Meshaal.

Osama Hamdan

Osama Hamdan, a member of Hamas's politburo, has led Hamas's branch office in Beirut, Lebanon since 1998, and has been a SDGT since August 2003. He was born in 1965 in the Bureij refugee camp in Gaza, but became active in Islamist movements while a student and young professional in Jordan and Kuwait. He relocated to Beirut after having spent six years during the 1990s based in Iran.

Hamdan often represents Hamas in Palestinian factional talks with Fatah and in discussions with Western officials. He and Mahmoud al Zahar have reportedly met periodically with former U.S. officials since 2009.

In Gaza

Ismail Haniyeh

Ismail Haniyeh is Hamas's "prime minister" in Gaza.

Haniyeh was born in or around 1955 in the Shati refugee camp in the Gaza Strip. In 1989, he was imprisoned for three years by Israeli authorities for participation in the first intifada. Following his release in 1992, he was deported to Lebanon along with approximately 400 other Hamas activists, but was eventually allowed to return to Gaza in 1993.[163] Upon his return, he was appointed dean of the Islamic University, and became the leader of Hamas's student movement. He was closely associated with Hamas co-founder and spiritual leader Sheikh Ahmed Yassin, and, following the assassination of Yassin and much of the Hamas leadership in 2004, became a prominent Hamas leader in Gaza.

Haniyeh favored Hamas's participation in the 2006 PLC elections, and headed the Hamas list of candidates. Following Hamas's victory, he served as PA prime minister from March 2006 until June 2007. Following Hamas's takeover of Gaza and its dismissal from the PA government in the West Bank, Hamas has continued to insist that Haniyeh is the PA prime minister, and he is treated as such in Gaza. Some observers believe that Haniyeh is more responsive to political realities than Hamas's leadership-in-exile, and use this rationale to argue that Haniyeh and/or other Gaza-based Hamas leaders might be persuaded to moderate their goals and tactics, even though he continues to advocate violent resistance against Israel. In Palestinian opinion polls for hypothetical presidential elections, Haniyeh consistently gets the most support among Hamas leaders, and sometimes runs close to Mahmoud Abbas in head-to-head pairings.

---

[163] See footnote 143.

Mahmoud al Zahar

Mahmoud al Zahar, is a medical doctor born in 1945 and based in Gaza, and also was one of the 400-plus deportees to Lebanon in 1992. Thought to have close ties with the politburo in Damascus, Zahar appears to have played a key role in the decision for Hamas to participate in the 2006 PLC elections. After being elected to the PLC, he served as foreign minister from 2006-2007 in the Hamas-led PA government, and continues to serve in that capacity for the Hamas-led regime in Gaza. He is one of the most outspoken members of Hamas's Gaza leadership with international media.

Ahmed Yousef

Ahmed Yousef (born 1950 in Gaza) is deputy foreign minister and a prominent media spokesman for the Hamas-led regime. Yousef lived in the United States from the 1980s until his return to Gaza around 2005. While a U.S. resident, Yousef earned multiple graduate degrees, and then served as director of the allegedly Hamas-linked United Association for Studies and Research in northern Virginia and as editor-in-chief of the *Middle East Affairs Journal*. One journalist has described Yousef's role in Hamas as follows:

> On the one hand, some people regard him as the representative of the moderate face of the movement capable of interacting with the world, while others believe his proposals are different to those held by the rest of the movement's leadership.... In any case, we are confronted by a talented man who bears the ideology of Hamas and deals with the media in an 'American' manner.[164]

Fathi Hamad

Fathi Hamad (born 1961 in Gaza) is the Hamas-led regime's interior minister, with charge over the regime's security forces. He became interior minister in 2009 after his predecessor Said Siyam was killed in an Israeli airstrike during Operation Cast Lead. Previously, he was the director of Hamas's public affairs department, which includes Hamas's Al Aqsa satellite television channel. He was elected to the PLC in 2006.

Hamad is thought by many to be a proponent of using both media and the security forces to effect greater Islamization of Gaza, although he has issued contradictory statements on the subject. A statement he made in 2008 has fueled allegations by Israel and others that Hamas uses civilians in Gaza as "human shields" to enable its militancy.[165]

---

[164] Osama Al-Essa, "The Smiling Face of Hamas," *Asharq Alawsat* (English edition), July 14, 2007, available at http://aawsat.com/english/news.asp?section=3&id=9575.

[165] Israel Ministry of Foreign Affairs, "Video: Hamas uses civilians as a means to achieving military goals," January 11, 2009, available at http://www.mfa.gov.il/MFA/Terrorism-+Obstacle+to+Peace/Hamas+war+against+Israel/Video_civilians_military_goals_Jan+2009.htm

Military Leaders in Gaza

Ahmed al Jaabari

Ahmed al Jaabari is thought to be the Gaza-based commander of the Izz Al Din al Qassam Brigades, Hamas's military wing. Jaabari, who has reportedly escaped multiple assassination attempts, does not make public appearances. Muhammad Deif, Jaabari's predecessor (and possibly still his equal or superior), has kept an even lower profile in recent years, possibly as the result of injury from a 2006 Israeli airstrike.[166]

Raed al Atar

Raed al Atar is the commander of the Rafah company of the Qassam Brigades. His command is important due to Rafah being the destination point for the smuggling tunnels from Egypt. Reports claim that Atar authorized the August 2010 firing of Grad-style rockets from the Sinai Peninsula at Eilat, Israel and Aqaba, Jordan, possibly raising questions about Atar's accountability and leverage within the Qassam Brigades chain of command and Hamas political-military structure.

---

[166] Yaakov Katz, "Meet the Hamas military leadership," *jpost.com*, December 22, 2008.

Appendix D. Congressional Actions Pertaining to Hamas

Table D-1. Current Legislation Pertaining to Hamas

Item	Brief Description	Disposition
Consolidated Appropriations Act, 2010 (P.L. 111-117)	Prohibits U.S. aid to Hamas and its affiliates and to any PA government with Hamas ministers unless all government ministers accept the Section 620K (from P.L. 109-446) principles: (1) recognition of the "Jewish state of Israel's right to exist," (2) acceptance of previous Israeli-Palestinian agreements.	Enacted December 16, 2009 Extended through December 3, 2010 by Continuing Appropriations Act, 2011 (P.L. 111-242)
Palestinian Anti-Terrorism Act of 2006 (P.L. 109-446)	Places various conditions and restrictions on U.S. aid intended for a "Hamas-controlled Palestinian Authority," including the Section 620K principles. Permits U.S. aid to be provided to non-Hamas-controlled branches of the PA under certain conditions.	Enacted December 21, 2006
Syria Accountability and Lebanese Sovereignty Restoration Act of 2003 (P.L. 108-175)	Requires President to levy sanctions against Syria unless he/she certifies that Syria has met certain conditions, with an end to support and safe haven for Hamas being one of them.	Enacted December 12, 2003
Iran Sanctions Act (originally titled the Iran and Libya Sanctions Act of 1996) (P.L. 104-172, as amended, including by P.L. 107-24, P.L. 109-293, and P.L. 111-195)	Requires President to levy sanctions against Iran and entities that engage in certain transactions unless he/she certifies that Iran has met certain conditions, with Iran's removal from the U.S. list of state sponsors of terrorism being one of them.	Enacted August 5, 1996 Most recently amended July 1, 2010 by Comprehensive Iran Sanctions, Divestment, and Accountability Act of 2010 (P.L. 111-195)

Table D-2. Selected Bills and Resolutions Pertaining to Hamas

Item	Brief Description	Disposition
S.Res. 571	Calls for the immediate and unconditional release of Israeli soldier Gilad Shalit held captive by Hamas, and for other purposes.	Passed Senate June 28, 2010 (Unanimous consent)
H.Res. 1359	Calls for the immediate and unconditional release of Israeli soldier Gilad Shalit, who is held captive by Hamas, and for other purposes.	Passed House June 24, 2010 (Voice vote)

Item	Brief Description	Disposition
UNRWA Humanitarian Accountability Act (H.R. 5065)	Would withhold U.S. contributions to UNRWA unless Secretary of State certifies every 180 days that (1) no UNRWA official or employee belongs to a terrorist organization, engages in incitement, or uses his/her position for political purposes; (2) no UNRWA recipient of funds or loans belongs to a terrorist organization; (3) UNRWA facilities and educational materials are not used by terrorist organizations or for purposes of incitement; (4) UNRWA implements vetting and oversight mechanisms and submits to regular independent third-party audits; and (5) UNRWA is not affiliated with financial institutions believed to be engaged or complicit in terrorist financing or money laundering.	Referred to House Foreign Affairs Committee April 20, 2010
	Would limit U.S. annual contributions to UNRWA to the lesser of (1) 22% of UNRWA's budget, (2) the largest annual contribution made by an Arab League member state, (3) a contribution that makes the U.S. percentage contribution to UNRWA's budget equal to the U.S. percentage contribution to the U.N. High Commissioner for Refugees' budget.	
H.R. 2278	Would seek to make it U.S. policy to urge all parties with influence over satellite transmissions to halt broadcasts of Hamas-run Al Aqsa TV and similar channels (including Hezbollah's Al Manar TV) and to name as SDGTs satellite providers that do not halt such broadcasts.	Passed House December 8, 2009 (395-3) Referred to Senate Foreign Relations Committee
	Would also require an annual presidential report to Congress on "anti-American incitement to violence" that would include a country-by-country breakdown of (1) all media outlets that engage in such incitement and (2) all satellite providers that carry programming classified as such incitement.	
H.Res. 867	Calls on the President and the Secretary of State to oppose unequivocally any endorsement or further consideration of the Report of the United Nations Fact Finding Mission on the Gaza Conflict (also known as the Goldstone Report) in multilateral fora.	Passed House November 3, 2009 (344-36)

Item	Brief Description	Disposition
H.Con.Res. 29	Expresses the sense of Congress that the United Nations should take immediate steps to improve the transparency and accountability of UNRWA to ensure that it is not providing funding, employment, or other support to terrorists.	Referred to House Foreign Affairs Committee January 28, 2009
H.Res. 34	Recognizes Israel's right to defend itself against attacks from Gaza, reaffirming the United States' strong support for Israel, and supporting the Israeli-Palestinian peace process	Passed House January 9, 2009 (390-5)
S.Res. 10	Recognizes the right of Israel to defend itself against attacks from Gaza, reaffirming the United States' strong support for Israel in its battle with Hamas, and supporting the Israeli-Palestinian peace process.	Passed Senate January 8, 2009 (Unanimous consent)
H.Res. 1069	Condemns Hamas's Al Aqsa TV (among other Middle East TV channels, including Hezbollah's Al Manar) for anti-Israel, anti-Semitic, and anti-U.S. incitement; calling upon satellite TV providers Arabsat (Arab League-owned, Saudi-based) and Eutelsat (privately owned, France-based) to cease transmitting Al Aqsa programming.	Passed House September 9, 2008 (409-1)
H.Res. 951	Condemns the ongoing Palestinian rocket attacks on Israeli civilians by Hamas and other Palestinian terrorist organizations, and for other purposes.	Passed House March 5, 2008 (404-1)
S.Res. 92	Calls for the immediate and unconditional release of soldiers of Israel held captive by Hamas and Hezbollah.	Passed Senate April 12, 2007 (Unanimous consent)
H.Res. 107	Calls for the immediate and unconditional release of Israeli soldiers held captive by Hamas and Hezbollah, and for other purposes	Passed House March 13, 2007 (Voice vote)
H.Res. 921	Condemns the recent attacks against the State of Israel, holding terrorists and their state sponsors accountable for such attacks, supporting Israel's right to defend itself, and for other purposes.	Passed House July 20, 2006 (410-8)
S.Res. 534	Condemns Hezbollah and Hamas and their state sponsors and supporting Israel's exercise of its right to self-defense.	Passed Senate July 18, 2006 (Voice vote)

Item	Brief Description	Disposition
H.Con.Res. 338	Expresses the sense of Congress regarding the activities of Islamist terrorist organizations in the Western Hemisphere.	Passed House June 12, 2006 (364-0) Referred to Senate Foreign Relations Committee
S.Con.Res. 79	Expresses the sense of Congress that no United States assistance should be provided directly to the Palestinian Authority if any representative political party holding a majority of parliamentary seats within the Palestinian Authority maintains a position calling for the destruction of Israel.	Passed Senate February 1, 2006 (Unanimous consent) Passed House February 15, 2006 (418-1)
H.Res. 575	Asserts that Hamas and other terrorist organizations should not participate in elections held by the Palestinian Authority, and for other purposes.	Passed House December 16, 2005 (397-17)
S.Res. 82	Urges the European Union to add Hezbollah to the European Union's wide-ranging list of terrorist organizations (partly because of Hezbollah's support for Hamas)	Passed Senate April 29, 2005 (Unanimous consent)
H.Res. 101	Urges the European Union to add Hezbollah to the European Union's wide-ranging list of terrorist organizations (partly because of Hezbollah's support for Hamas)	Passed House March 14, 2005 (380-3)
S.Res. 393	Endorses progress toward realizing the vision of two states living side by side in peace and security, as a real contribution toward peace, and as important steps under the Road Map; supports efforts to continue working with others in the international community, to build the capacity and will of Palestinian institutions to fight terrorism, dismantle terrorist organizations, and prevent the areas from which Israel has withdrawn from posing a threat to the security of Israel; and for other purposes.	Passed Senate June 24, 2004 (95-3)
H.Con.Res. 460	Supports continuing efforts with others in the international community to build the capacity and will of Palestinian institutions to fight terrorism, dismantle terrorist organizations, and prevent the areas from which Israel has withdrawn from posing a threat to the security of Israel; and for other purposes.	Passed House June 23, 2004 (407-9) Referred to Senate Foreign Relations Committee

Item	Brief Description	Disposition
H.Res. 294	Recognizes and respects Israel's right to fight terrorism and acknowledges Israel's fight against terrorism as part of the global war against terrorism; calls on all states to cease recognition of and political and material support for any Palestinian and other terrorist groups; calls on all states immediately to establish effective mechanisms to ensure that funding from private citizens cannot be directed to terrorist groups for any purpose whatsoever, including ostensible humanitarian purposes; calls on all states to provide support to the Palestinian Authority in its effort to confront and fight terror; and for other purposes.	Passed House June 25, 2003 (399-5)
H.Res. 61	Urges the Palestinian leadership to abide by its commitments made to the United States and to Israel and urges the Palestinian people to act on President Bush's call of June 24, 2002, to dismantle the terrorist infrastructure, end incitement to violence in official media, elect new leaders not compromised by terror, and embrace democracy; and for other purposes.	Passed House February 11, 2003 (411-2)
H.Res. 392	Expresses solidarity with Israel as it takes necessary steps to provide security to its people by dismantling the terrorist infrastructure in the Palestinian areas; condemns the recent wave of Palestinian suicide bombings; demands that the Palestinian Authority at last fulfill its commitment to dismantle the terrorist infrastructure in the Palestinian areas, including any such infrastructure associated with PLO and Palestinian Authority entities tied directly to Yasir Arafat; urges all Arab states to declare their unqualified opposition to all forms of terrorism, including suicide bombing; and for other purposes.	Passed House May 2, 2002 (352-21)

Item	Brief Description	Disposition
H.Con.Res. 280	Expresses solidarity with Israel in the fight against terrorism; expresses outrage at the ongoing Palestinian terrorist campaign (especially the attacks of December 1-2, 2001 that killed 26 and injured at least 175) and insists that the Palestinian Authority take all steps necessary to end it; urges the President to insist that all countries harboring, materially supporting, or acquiescing in the private support of Palestinian terrorist groups end all such support, dismantle the infrastructure of such groups, and bring all terrorists within their borders to justice; and for other purposes.	Passed House December 5, 2001 (384-11) Referred to Senate Foreign Relations Committee
S.Con.Res. 88	Essentially similar to H.Con.Res. 280.	Passed Senate December 5, 2001 (Unanimous consent) and held at the desk
S.Amdt. 3528 *(to Foreign Operations, Export Financing, and Related Programs Appropriations Act, 1999 (S. 2334))*	Expresses the finding of the Senate that according to the Department of State, Iran continues to support international terrorism, providing training, financing and weapons to such terrorist groups as Hezbollah, Islamic Jihad, and Hamas.	Passed Senate September 2, 1998 (Voice vote) S. 2334 passed Senate September 2, 1998 (90-3)
S.Res. 228	Condemns terror attacks in Israel.	Passed Senate February 29, 1996 (Voice vote)
H.Con.Res. 149	Condemns terror attacks in Israel; urging PA President/PLO Chairman Yasser Arafat to (1) apprehend and punish the perpetrators of terror attacks; (2) eliminate the terrorist structure and terrorist activities of Hamas.	Passed House March 12, 1996 (406-0) Referred to Senate Foreign Relations Committee

Appendix E. Selected Bibliography on Hamas

Biersteker, Thomas J. and Sue E. Eckert (eds.), *Countering the Financing of Terrorism*, Routledge, New York, 2008.

Brown, Nathan J. and Amr Hamzawy, "Hamas: Battling to Blend Religion, Politics, Resistance, and Governance," *Between Religion and Politics*, Carnegie Endowment for International Peace, Washington, DC, 2010.

Chehab, Zaki, *Inside Hamas: The Untold Story of the Militant Islamic Movement*, Nation Books, New York, 2007.

Cohen, Yoram and Matthew Levitt (with Becca Wasser), *Deterred but Determined: Salafi-Jihadi Groups in the Palestinian Arena*, Washington Institute for Near East Policy PolicyFocus #99, January 2010, available at http://www.washingtoninstitute.org/pubPDFs/ PolicyFocus%2099.pdf.

Cohen, Yoram and Jeffrey White, *Hamas in Combat: The Military Performance of the Palestinian Islamic Resistance Movement*, Washington Institute for Near East Policy, Policy Focus #97, October 2009, available at http://www.washingtoninstitute.org/pubPDFs/ PolicyFocus97.pdf.

Gold, Dore, et al. (eds.), *Iran, Hizbullah, Hamas and the Global Jihad : A New Conflict Paradigm for the West*, Jerusalem Center for Public Affairs, Jerusalem, 2007.

Gunning, Jeroen, *Hamas in Politics: Democracy, Religion, Violence*, Columbia University Press, New York, 2008.

Hroub, Khaled, *Hamas: A Beginner's Guide*, Pluto Press, Ann Arbor, Michigan, 2006.

Human Rights Watch, *Internal Fight: Palestinian Abuses in Gaza and the West Bank*, July 29, 2008, available at http://www.hrw.org/en/reports/2008/07/29/internal-fight-0.

Human Rights Watch, *Rockets from Gaza: Harm to Civilians from Palestinian Armed Groups' Rocket Attacks*, August 6, 2009, available at http://www.hrw.org/en/reports/2009/08/06/ rockets-gaza-0.

Human Rights Watch, *Under Cover of War: Hamas Political Violence in Gaza*, April 20, 2009, available at http://www.hrw.org/node/82366.

Jensen, Michael Irving, *Political Ideology of Hamas: A Grassroots Perspective*, Palgrave Macmillan, New York, 2009.

Kepel, Gilles, *Jihad: The Trail of Political Islam*, Harvard University Press (Belknap Press), Cambridge, Massachusetts, 2003.

Levitt, Matthew, *Hamas: Politics, Charity, and Terrorism in the Service of Jihad*, Yale University Press, New Haven, Connecticut, 2006.

Levitt, Matthew and Michael Jacobson, *The Money Trail: Finding, Following, and Freezing Terrorist Finances*, Washington Institute for Near East Policy, Policy Focus #89, November 2008, available at http://www.washingtoninstitute.org/pubPDFs/PolicyFocus89.pdf.

Levy, Gideon, *The Punishment of Gaza*, Verso Books, New York, 2010.

Lia, Brynjar, *Building Arafat's Police: The Politics of International Police Assistance in the Palestinian Territories after the Oslo Agreement*, Ithaca Press, Reading, UK, 2007.

Lia, Brynjar, *A Police Force Without a State: A History of the Palestinian Security Forces in the West Bank and Gaza*, Ithaca Press, Reading, UK, 2006.

Milton-Edwards, Beverley and Stephen Farrell, *Hamas: The Islamic Resistance Movement*, Polity Press, Malden, Massachusetts, 2010.

Mishal, Shaul and Avraham Sela, *The Palestinian Hamas: Vision, Violence, and Coexistence*, Columbia University Press, New York, 2006.

McGeough, Paul, *Kill Khalid: The Failed Mossad Assassination and the Rise of Hamas*, The New Press, New York, 2009.

Nüsse, Andrea, *Muslim Palestine: The Ideology of Hamas*, Harwood Academic Publishers, Amsterdam, 1998.

Perry, Mark, *Talking to Terrorists: Why America Must Engage with Its Enemies*, Basic Books, New York, 2010.

Rubin, Barry (ed.), *The Muslim Brotherhood: The Organization and Policies of a Global Islamist Movement*, Palgrave Macmillan, New York, 2010.

Schanzer, Jonathan, *Hamas vs. Fatah: The Struggle for Palestine*, Palgrave Macmillan, New York, 2008.

Shachar, Nathan, *The Gaza Strip: Its History and Politics: From the Pharoahs to the Israeli Invasion of 2009*, Sussex Academic Press, Eastbourne, UK, 2010.

Shamir, Jacob and Khalil Shikaki, *Palestinian and Israeli Public Opinion: The Public Imperative in the Second Intifada*, Indiana University Press, Bloomington, Indiana, 2010.

Tamimi, Azzam, *Hamas: A History from Within*, Olive Branch Press, Northampton, Massachusetts, 2007.

United Nations, *Report of the U.N. Fact Finding Mission on the Gaza Conflict* (the "Goldstone Report"), September 25, 2009, available at http://www2.ohchr.org/english/bodies/hrcouncil/specialsession/9/FactFindingMission.htm.

Yousef, Mosab Hassan with Ron Brackin, *Son of Hamas*, Salt River, Carol Stream, Illinois, 2010.

Zuhur, Sherifa, *Hamas and Israel: Conflicting Strategies of Group-Based Politics*, U.S. Army War College Strategic Studies Institute, Carlisle, Pennsylvania, December 2008.

Author Contact Information

Jim Zanotti
Analyst in Middle Eastern Affairs
jzanotti@crs.loc.gov, 7-1441

Acknowledgments

Brent Cottrell contributed significant research and writing assistance to this report during his internship at CRS in the summer of 2010.

www.ingramcontent.com/pod-product-compliance
Lightning Source LLC
Chambersburg PA
CBHW081853280526
45789CB00007B/2687